PIERCING TH

CENTENNIAL PUBLICATION
To Mark the First Ascent of Mt Cook
Christmas Day 1894

PIERCING THE CLOUDS

Tom Fyfe:
First to Climb
Mt Cook

John Haynes

HP
HAZARD PRESS
publishers

ACKNOWLEDGEMENTS

I wish to express my thanks to several members of the Fyfe family who willingly helped me to understand personal aspects of Thomas Camperdown Fyfe: Noreen Forde (niece), Nelson Fyfe (grandson), Lois Fyfe (great-granddaughter), Audrey Preece and Dorothy Bishell (granddaughters) and especially his son, Malcolm Fyfe, whom I was able to interview.

I would like to record my gratitude for the many kinds of assistance I have received from numerous other people. In particular I wish to thank:

Andrew Anderson, Bob Barrack, Olive Bunce, Gotlieb Braun-Elwert, Mike Browne, Brenda Carter, Gar Graham, Dave Hughes, Leon Grice, Stephen Grice, Graham Langton, Hugh Logan, Peter McCormick, Colin Monteath, John Small, and Gavin Wills.
I also wish to acknowledge the help I received from the following organisations:

Aoraki Corporation, National Library, Canterbury Museum, Department of Conservation, Federated Mountain Clubs of New Zealand, Hocken Library, National Archives, New Zealand Alpine Club and *Otago Daily Times*.

To Fiona, Michael, Helen,
Olive and Joe

CONTENTS

Mt Cook - ridges and faces

NORTH RIDGE
EAST RIDGE
WEST RIDGE
SOUTH RIDGE
EARLE RIDGE
ZURBRIGGEN R
BOWIE R
Linda Glacier

Fyfes Route
Sheila Face
High Peak 12 349'
East Face
Hooker Face
Middle Peak 12 210'
Caroline Face
Low Peak 11 787'
South Face

Heights as at time of first ascent

N

Terra Nova Pass
Mt D'Archiac
Godley Glacier
Godley River
DIVIDE
MAIN
Whataroa River

Lendenfeld Saddle
Hochstetter Dome
Tasman Saddle
Whymper Gl
Elie de Beaumont
Mt Darwin
Spencer Gl
Minarets
De La Beche
Graham Saddle
Rudolf Glacier
Josef Glacier
Franz
Fox Glacier
Glacier Peak
Mt Haidinger
De La Beche Gl
Malte Brun
Malte Brun
MALTE BRUN
Murchison River
MURCHISON
LIEBIG RANGE
Rutherford Pass
Cass River
Mt Biretta

Grand Plateau
Linda Gl
Glacier Dome
Mt Cook
Tasman Glacier
Ball
Ball Pass
Mt Tasman
Mt Dampier
Mt Hicks
Harper Saddle
La Perouse
Empress Gl
Nolline
Raureka Peak
Hooker R
Copland Pass
Stocking Stm
Tasman River
Strauchon Gl
Dilemma Peak
Copland Gl
Sefton Blv
Kea Pt
HERMITAGE
Mt Sealy
The Footstool
Mt Sefton
Douglas Gl
Maunga Ma
Mueller Glacier
McKerrow Gl
Fyfe Pass
Mt Montgomery
Douglas Pass
MAIN DIVIDE
Copland River
Landsborough River

Glacier
Ridge
Hut

Drawn by Graphics/Draughting Department of Conservation

8

INTRODUCTION

For thousands of years the great peaks of New Zealand's Southern Alps stood sublime, unknown to humans, and inhabited only by kea flying guardian over the icy landscape. Glaciers of immense size advanced and retreated, carving out huge valleys and broad terraces, and on the West Coast sometimes reaching the sea. Lakes formed at the foot of the glaciers, and on the terraces vegetation grew that was capable of sustaining life.

To Aotearoa's earliest inhabitants this vast inland area was a place for summer hunting as it contained moa in large numbers. Maori also named many of the geographic features: the three lakes — Tekapo, Pukaki and Ohau — and the peaks, notably the highest, which they called Aoraki, commemorating a legendary navigator. In 1851 it was also given a European name when Captain J.L. Stokes, commander of HMS *Acheron* during a survey of the West Coast, sighted 'a most stupendous mountain' and named it Mt Cook in honour of another famous navigator.

Mt Cook, however, is but one of many high mountains in the area. For mile upon mile huge rock and ice peaks thrust upwards from two to ten thousand feet, notable among them Mts Tasman, Dampier, La Perouse and Malte Brun. From this massif of rock, snow and ice, the Fox and Franz Josef Glaciers fall spectacularly down to the West Coast. To the east the Tasman, Mueller, Murchison and Hooker Glaciers feed Pukaki, the largest of the trio of lakes, while the Godley Glacier provides the turquoise water that makes Tekapo so distinctive.

The first useful map of this region of the Alps was drawn by Julius von Haast. Several years previously he had done considerable exploration in the Alps, beginning with a commission from the Canterbury Provincial Council in 1861 when he led a party which first explored the headwaters of the Ashburton and Rangitata rivers. In 1862 he then spent three months further south, assessing the prospects of discovering gold in the Mackenzie basin and identifying prominent features. Besides naming features after notable European scientists, such as De la Beche and Elie de Beaumont, he honoured his superiors by identifying the Godley Glacier, the Godley River and the Moorhouse Range which overlooks the site of the Hermitage, together with its highest peak, Mt Sefton. Edward Sealy also contributed to knowledge of the region, and to von Haast's map. A surveyor by profession and also a keen photographer, in 1867 he traversed the whole length of the Mueller Glacier, and two years later made his way up the Hooker Glacier as far as the Empress Glacier and also up the Tasman Glacier as far as the turn known as De la Beche corner.

For approximately fifteen years after von Haast's and Sealy's pioneering work the only visitors to the Mt Cook region appear to have been camping parties and their families on sightseeing outings. However, the tourist potential of the area was noted by Sir George Bowen, Governor of New Zealand 1868-1873, when he camped close to the site of the present Hermitage. To encourage interest in climbing nearby summits, he offered assistance to any member of the Alpine Club in England who attempted to climb Mt Cook. No one had done any high-level mountaineering in New Zealand, and our highest peak first attracted attention from the British. This was to be expected, as between 1854 and 1865, the so-called golden age of mountaineering, English climbers with European guides had made the first ascents of all but eight of the thirty-nine major peaks in Europe. Looking elsewhere for equivalent challenges after those successes, they turned their attention first to the Himalaya and the Andes, and eventually the Southern Alps.

Responding to the Governor's offer, an Irish clergyman, Rev. William Green, made the first attempt on Mt Cook. He had begun his climbing career in Europe in 1869, and in 1882 he came to New Zealand for the specific purpose of making the first ascent of Mt Cook. Led by Ulrich Kaufmann, a Swiss guide renowned for his skill in ice climbing, and in the company of another Swiss, Emil Boss, Green explored several possible approaches to the peak. They eventually settled on a route from the north-eastern approaches, using a camp they established on the Haast

The first party to attempt Mt Cook: left to right: Ulrich Kaufmann, Rev. William Green, Emil Boss. 1882.
Photo: G.E. Mannering

Ridge and via a glacier which Green named Linda after his wife. Kaufmann's route was a long one and required a large amount of step cutting.

At first the weather boded well, and on 1 March 1882 Kaufmann led the party across the vast basin then called the Grand Plateau toward the head of the Linda Glacier. However, as they ascended higher the step cutting that was required used up precious daylight hours. Then the wind rose, and by 5.30 pm it had such force that they could barely hear one another's shouts. So although they were high on the peak Green retreated. Descending

F.F.C. Huddleston. Surveyor, artist and conservationist, he built and managed the first Hermitage and helped to ensure the reservation of land that was later incorporated into Mt Cook National Park.
Source: *Cyclopedia of New Zealand: Nelson-Westland*

to a small rock ledge, they stood out the night stormbound until recommencing their descent in the morning.

On Green's return to Christchurch his achievements were celebrated with a series of dinners and social engagements. The party was photographed by George Mannering, whose imagination was fired by the the trio's exploits and by the possibility of climbing Mt Cook. He believed that 'the apathy of the Colonials regarding the scenic marvels of their country was aroused' by Green's enterprise. New Zealanders now began to take an interest in the mountain regions. In 1884 the artist F.F.C. Huddleston built a hotel at Mt Cook which he then sold to a group of South Canterbury businessmen who had formed the Mt Cook Hermitage Company. Until 1895 this provided accommodation. Mannering made the first of several visits to the area in 1886, and together with a few pioneering alpinists explored the glaciers and gradually revealed more and more of the topography. They also wrote articles for daily and weekly newspapers, so that the general public became more aware of the attractions of the Mt Cook region.

In 1889 earlier government surveys were extended. T.N. Brodrick, the district surveyor, attained both the saddle at the head of the Mueller Glacier (later named Barron Saddle) and the saddle connecting the Murchison and Classen Glaciers. With his assistant, Sladden, Brodrick also climbed to the lower summit of Hochstetter Dome, the highest peak of which had been reached by Dr. R. von Lendenfeld, his wife and a porter, H. Dew, in 1883.

In the late 1880s George Mannering and his friend, Marmaduke Dixon, made several attempts to climb Mt Cook. In 1890, after a very long climb on the same route that Green's party had used, they reached approximately the same point that Green had reached. Mannering reported their anguished decision: 'At about 5 pm we had reached an altitude of 12,000 ft. The rope was frozen hard and we were very much exhausted. We were now less than 200 feet from the summit. All the difficulties were overcome and it only remained to cut steps for an hour at most to reach the mathematical top. Had we stopped at that hour, however, we should have been compelled to remain all night, and as that probably meant leaving our bones there we decided to return and

Mt Cook's High Peak rises 4,000 feet sheer from the Hooker Glacier, dominating its neighbours. Fyfe ascended and descended both the North Ridge (left), and Earles Route (centre).

Photo: Colin Monteath, Hedgehog House

attempt to reach our tracks at the head of the Linda Glacier before dark.'[1] They finally reached their camp at 2.45 am, having climbed for twenty-three and a half hours without a halt.

Mt Cook remained unclimbed, as did all the major peaks in the region. The exploration of the glaciers and the various approaches to these peaks continued, however, and with Mannering's journey up the Murchison Glacier and Arthur Harper's climb to the head of the Hooker in 1890 with R. Blakiston and W. Beadel, the

13

M.J. Dixon and G.E. Mannering in 1890, who by then had made several attempts to climb Mt Cook.
Photo: Peter Graham

tangled topography of the area was gradually being more clearly revealed.

The opening of the Hermitage and the improvement of travel arrangements meant that a permanent base was provided from which climbers could work. The first manager at the Hermitage, Frank Huddleston, and then Jack Adamson later, helped to interpret the area. They took an active interest in climbing, and the owners, the Mt Cook Hermitage Company Ltd, provided a guiding service to the glaciers. However, access beyond the Hermitage presented formidable obstacles for early climbers. The first was the swirling water in the rocky bed of the Hooker River which drains both the Mueller and the Hooker Glaciers. Until the later installation of a wire cage, provisions had to be taken across on horseback through a ford which could be deep and swift during the summer.

T.N. Brodrick, government surveyor for the district, camping with his family. His contribution to mapping and planning in the Mt Cook area, especially his overseeing of roads, tracks and huts, is commemorated in two features, Brodrick Peak and Brodrick Pass.

Source: Canterbury Museum

Another deterrent was the heavy swagging that had to be done through the scrub and rocky moraine of the Tasman valley. Trackless until 1891, this approach was a tedious journey, sapping energy and using food resources. Pioneering climbers had to camp in the open at the mercy of often sudden and violent changes in weather. There were no huts at all until, under the supervision of T.N. Brodrick, Ball Hut was built by the government in 1891 at the junction of the Ball and Tasman Glaciers. It gave shelter to climbers near the Tasman Glacier and overnight accommodation for tourists. Some eight miles further up the Tasman at the De la Beche corner there was another shelter, a natural one. Crouched between the Rudolf and the Tasman glaciers was a gigantic boulder, with a cavity underneath. Sometimes referred to as Harper's hut, but later as the De la Beche bivouac, it provided excellent protection in storms and its location made Mt De la Beche a goal for climbers.

At the beginning of the last decade of the nineteenth century this was the state of knowledge of the Mt Cook region, these were the achievements of climbers and these were the conditions they faced. In 1890 there arrived from Timaru, on his first visit to the region, a young man sent to work at the Hermitage. Tom Fyfe had never climbed before, but he soon established an outstanding reputation as a mountaineer and later as a guide and explorer. Through his personal qualities and inventiveness he brought new skills to alpine climbing and he fashioned an outstanding record of new routes and first ascents.

1   *Weekly Press,* 17 December 1890.

1

TIMARU ORIGINS

Tom Fyfe's father, Thomas Webster Fyfe, a Scot, had arrived in Timaru in 1862 on the *Echunga,* the second ship to bring immigrants for the new South Canterbury settlement. He immediately looked for work as a painter and glazier, the trade he had learned in his native Dundee before moving to London. He married Jane Craigie, also of Scottish descent. Her brother, James Craigie, had a successful plumbing business, became mayor of Timaru in 1905 and was later elected member of Parliament for the district. The family name has long been commemorated in a prominent avenue in the city.

By the standards of the day, Thomas and Jane Fyfe were an educated and cultured couple who wanted the same for their children. They were also ambitious. Soon after his arrival, Thomas had paid £60 to a Mr Proctor for his painting and glazing business, the price including a section of land with a hut on it as well as the stock-in-trade and goodwill. Later Thomas bought a section in Heaton Street in Government Town and with help he built a large three-bedroomed house of cob, roofed with shingle. It was in this house on 23 June 1870 that Thomas Camperdown Fyfe was born, the third of the eleven children borne by Jane between 1868 and 1888. There were two older sisters, Margaret and Jane (Jeannie), and the younger children were, in order, Jessie, Isabella (Bella), Evelyn, Alfred, William, Minnie Wai-iti, Charles and Christopher.

Thomas Camperdown Fyfe, aged four years.
Source: T.M. Fyfe

As the family's size and fortunes increased, the house was extended by four more rooms and another storey, this time using timber construction. Later, other additions were made. A well was dug and, by means of a force pump and pipes, water was supplied to other houses besides their own. The family business flourished, and Tom's father bought more sections and built houses or shops on them. One block next to the Lands Office was known as Fyfe's buildings. So the boy grew up in

Jane Fyfe (née Craigie), mother of Tom Fyfe.
Source: Dorothy Bishell and Noreen Forde

comparative comfort, although later in life he eschewed the accumulation of wealth.

True to their Scottish heritage, the Fyfe family believed in the value of formal education. Tom's father was fond of reciting the poems of Robbie Burns, and chaired the first meeting of the Wai-iti School Committee. In fact the first recorded meeting of that committee was held in their house on 31 December 1879, the stone school building having been erected that year. On 28 July 1880, at the age of ten, Tom attended as a first-day pupil, along with five of his sisters, Margaret, Jane, Isabella, Jessie and Evelyn. The school roll was thirty-six, and the teacher was a Cambridge graduate, Mr T.A. Walker.[1] Jessie and Evelyn Fyfe both became school teachers, and several of the children became prominent in musical circles in Timaru, one of the younger ones, Minnie Wai-iti, being regarded as particularly gifted in singing.

Home and school influences made Tom into a keen reader. As shown by what has survived of his written accounts, he developed a fluent use of language and a clear script. However, as an adult he often agonised over writing tasks. Once, having agreed to supply a report of a climb, he then regretted it, explaining to J.J. Kinsey, a fellow climbing enthusiast in Christchurch, that he 'would rather top a 10,000 footer than write a page'.[2] This may explain why he never wrote a manuscript about his achievements as was suggested to him by the London publishers Fisher Unwin.

The young town of Timaru and the surrounding region prospered, and in 1868 it was constituted as the province of South Canterbury. The Fyfe business flourished too, as did Craigie's plumbing business. By the age of fifteen Tom was described as fair-headed with sharp blue eyes and of sturdy build. Strong in the arms, he got considerable encouragement from his family because, although not keen on team sports, he was very competitive at individual events. He and his cousin, Alex Donn, would often try each other out with feats of strength and weightlifting. He became apprenticed to his uncle, and later as a fully qualified plumber his skill was much admired. In his

18

work he travelled widely around the town and in the surrounding district, going further and further afield — eventually to the Southern Alps.

As the eldest son of a large family, it is likely that some qualities of leadership were always expected of Tom Fyfe, and together with his reputedly relaxed and cheerful manner and all-round competence this seems to have enabled him to mix easily with people. The family's talent for music may have encouraged his social development, but he was also very independent. Cards were sometimes the evening recreation for the family — euchre, whist and cribbage. In 1897 Fyfe wrote that his climbing party, after twenty hours on the move, had sat up until after midnight playing whist.[3] He was as self-sufficient as he was socially at ease, and thus well able to appreciate silence and solitude. He once wrote that an advantage of climbing alone is that 'one is not distracted by the idle chatter of companions'.

James Craigie, MHR, MLC, Tom Fyfe's uncle and employer. Source: J. Glass

He was an excellent swimmer, but the sport in which he specialised was cycling. As leisure opportunities increased in the 1880s, there arose a corresponding interest in recreational and competitive sports — tennis parties, football and cricket matches, athletic and cycling races. In Timaru this was marked as early as 1876, the year in which the South Canterbury Caledonian Society held its first gathering. By 1889 the society had acquired a piece of land just to the south of the town for this purpose, and it has held its New Year's Day games there ever since. The programme included cycling, running, walking, wrestling, throwing the stone, the hammer and the caber, Scottish dancing, and bayonet exercises.

These gatherings began to attract crowds of 5,000 or more, often including a thousand visitors on morning trains from Fairlie, Ashburton and Oamaru. If they were fortunate with the weather, spectators could expect to be cooled by a sea breeze; but if a nor'wester blew, the only shelter from the heat was under parasols. They were well entertained by the various contests as well as by the Garrison Band which had marched from the Grosvenor Hotel accompanied by kilted Caledonians. The day was often rounded off by a public concert in the evening, with vocalists from as far away as Christchurch and Invercargill.

Cycling was given an enormous boost by the first cycle ride around the world. An American, Thomas Stevens, riding a fifty-six-inch wheeler, known then as an ordinary, but now as a penny-farthing, set off east from San Francisco on 22 April 1884, travelling across USA, Europe and Asia by road, track, camel trail and even watercourse, eventually reaching Yokohama and boarding a steamer for home on 17 December 1886.[4] Feats such as these, combined with the lure of prize money, attracted those men who, like Fyfe, were competitive and had a strong physique, especially if they had powerful legs. He joined the Timaru Tourist Club which organised club runs and record-breaking attempts at various distances. Evelyn Hosken wrote that in the time of the penny-farthing it took a real champion to get down to three minutes in the mile, and in the days when people made their own fun, attempts were made to ride up Le Cren Terrace in Timaru. The only one to accomplish this was Tom Fyfe. The gradient of that street has since been eased, but it still demands a substantial effort. Club rides were formal and colourful affairs. Members wore a uniform, usually a striped jacket set off by a ribbon or a badge, and the formation was led by the club captain, followed by members in order of seniority determined by performance, with the sub-captain bringing up the rear.

Racing the high bicycles required considerable nerve and good balance, attributes which Fyfe had from an early age. It was at the Caledonian sports in 1889 that he had his first notable success. Aged nineteen, he got the winner's purse of £4 in the three-mile race. A reporter for the *Timaru Herald* wrote, 'The race was conspicuous for the splendid riding of Fyfe (Tourist Club). He had the lead before two miles were covered and won well.'[5] The following year he was there again, this time beating McDonald and Hall from scratch in the one-mile race. The same reporter called the race a gift for Fyfe: he had everyone beaten in the third lap and pedalled in an easy winner for a prize of £2 10s. His victory was probably expected because of what he had done just a few days before in Christchurch.

Stafford Street, Timaru in the 1870s. Much of the commercial area was rebuilt in stone after a disastrous fire in 1868.
Source: South Canterbury Centennial Association

At a prestigious three-day inter-colonial meeting at Lancaster Park which began on Boxing Day 1890, Fyfe had shown skill and a tough competitive spirit against noted riders from elsewhere in New Zealand and also from Australia. In front of crowds of up to 8,000 people, he won the three-mile roadster handicap in fine style, headed off a determined challenge for first in a four-mile event, and won the final of the one-mile by half a dozen yards in a record time of 2 minutes 50.5 seconds. He also gained a highly creditable second in the two-mile roadster handicap, attracting attention by the way he wore down an opponent in the straight to defeat him by a couple of yards.[6] He went home with £10 in his pocket, quite a sum when a weekly wage was usually less than a quarter of that.

Although he never again competed with such intensity and success, Tom Fyfe never lost his love of cycling. In later years he covered many miles in Hastings on the kind of bicycle used today, known then as a safety bicycle. But something else happened in 1890 that turned out to be far more important for his future than cycling. He visited the Mount Cook area for the first time and made his first climbing trip in the Southern Alps. Thus began an interest that became a passion.

21

1   W. C. Charteris, *Cheerful Yesterdays,* (Timaru, 1979), p. 4.
2   T. C. Fyfe, letter to J. J. Kinsey, 27 November 1987, Alexander Turnbull Library.
3   *Ibid.*
4   F. Alderson, *Bicycling: a history,* (Davis and Charles), p. 41.
5   *Timaru Herald,* 3 January 1889.
6   *Weekly Press,* 3 January 1890.

2

FIRST TASTE OF CLIMBING

Since leaving school at fifteen Tom Fyfe had been gaining wide experience during his apprenticeship in all aspects of his trade. He could be relied upon to work in the solitude of the back country and to resolve problems unaided. In 1890 when a new wing was to be added to the cob building that served as the Hermitage at Mt Cook, his uncle sent him to do the plumbing work.

In those days the journey to the Hermitage from Timaru began with a train trip to Fairlie where there was a comfortable hotel in the town offering overnight accommodation. The coach which then took travellers on the two-day trip from Fairlie to Mt Cook lurched over barely formed tracks via Lake Tekapo and Lake Pukaki, finally turning up the south bank of the Tasman River and following it to the Hooker Valley. The road between Lake Pukaki and the Hermitage was improved in 1892 when Brodrick, the surveyor, oversaw the spending of £400 voted by the government, following representations by the hotel owners and the local member of Parliament.

The Christchurch-Dunedin express train at Timaru in the 1880s. This service, and the branch railway to Fairlie, opened up the South Canterbury hinterland to travellers.
Source: *South Canterbury: A Record of Settlement*

23

The railhead, at left, and the main street of Fairlie, gateway to the Mackenzie basin, 1880s.
Source: Mackenzie Historical Association

The coach journey was long and tiresome, the first day's run from Fairlie to Pukaki being fifty-six often dusty miles in hot weather, hauled by four horses that were changed several times. But there was a respite when the coach stopped at Lake Tekapo for lunch. The hotel's garden was only a few paces from the edge of the lake. Turquoise blue from its glacial sources, the lake was then the foreground of the same striking vista that can be seen today, the distant mountains rising out of the Godley Glacier forming a perfect backdrop. After the horses were changed the whole ensemble headed up the winding road which climbed away towards Lake Pukaki. From here, if the mountains were not covered in cloud, Tom Fyfe would have seen for the first time the astonishing spectacle of Mts Cook, Tasman and Malte Brun clustered together with the other large mountains of the region. Even from a distance of forty miles they seem to rise effortlessly from the Mackenzie basin.

After a long day's jolting ride Lake Pukaki came into view. It would be almost sunset by the time the passengers could climb off the coach and sit down to a meal. If the mountains were clear, people would be able to look across the lake and pick out the approximate line of the track where they would continue their journey up to the Hermitage. Early next morning they were on the way again. First though, the coach had to cross the Pukaki River on a ferry made of two whale-boats joined together by plank decking. (The bridge was not built until 1895.) Once

24

across, the driver guided his charges over the tussocks of Rhoborough Downs Station. From there the road was extremely rough with numerous large boulders, the only compensation being the views that changed as the travellers approached the mountains. Finally, as the coach drew away from the Tasman River the magnificent peaks of the upper Tasman Glacier could be seen, only to vanish as the coach turned abruptly left and wound its way up the short but spectacular valley of the Hooker, revealing straight ahead the colossal bulk of Mt Sefton and its spectacular icefalls. Of this view Julius von Haast wrote appreciatively: 'Alpine peaks appear everywhere glistening with snow and ice, frowning rocky precipices furrowing their sides and, above them all, the bold majestic Mt Cook stood out conspicuously. This is still more striking as this glorious mountain rises abruptly in the foreground for more than 10,000 feet above the broad valley.'[1]

There is no record of the exact date when Tom Fyfe first made this journey or of how long he spent working as a plumber at the Hermitage. Nor did he leave any written account of how and when he began climbing. For that it is necessary to rely upon a slim volume, *Aorangi*, by Malcolm Ross, which was published in 1892. Ross wrote that in 1890, having done a little climbing on Mt Earnslaw, he was staying at Mt Cook with his wife, intending to do some climbing. They spent some time on the Tasman Glacier and after talking with Frank Huddleston, the manager of the Hermitage, Ross decided to do a trip up onto the Mueller Glacier and then onto the Sealy Range, planning to climb Mt Sealy.

He started out next morning taking only some lunch and an alpenstock — a long iron-tipped stick for hill walking — accompanied by Huddleston's fox terrier eager for a mountain scramble. It was a glorious morning, with the head of the Hooker Glacier gleaming in the sunlight and with the long south ridge of Mt Cook still in shadow. Indeed, for a view of the Hooker area, the Sealy Range is the perfect vantage point. To add to the splendour and drama of such days, avalanches thunder down off Mt Sefton reminding climbers of the destructive power the mountains can unleash. On this day also the roof was being put

John Rutherford of the Mt Cook Company driving the Governor, Lord Onslow, to the Hermitage in 1889. The company's coaches, green with yellow trim, and drawn by black horses, presented a smart appearance.
Source: *South Canterbury: A Record of Settlement*

on to the new wing of the Hermitage, and in the clear silence the hammer blows echoed off the mountains and could be heard far up on the ranges.

As the sun rose higher in the sky the heat became intense. Like many climbers since who have gone this way, Ross stopped by one of the isolated mountain tarns at about 5,000 feet. He chanced to look up and was surprised to see someone on the rocks above him. He said, 'It turned out to be the plumber-lad who was engaged in works at the Hermitage and after depicting the projected expedition in glowing colours and offering to share my luncheon with him he was easily persuaded to accompany me.'[2]

When Ross wrote this account he did not name the plumber-lad, possibly because in 1892 Fyfe was not thought important

The whaleboat ferry takes a passenger coach across the Pukaki River in 1890, using a wire and the force of the current. In the background.is the old Pukaki Hotel.
Source: Collection of former Pukaki Inn.

enough to warrant a mention. But he came to know Fyfe very well and often climbed with him, and in his 1914 book, *A Climber in New Zealand,* Ross acknowledged Fyfe as one who was "destined to play no inconsiderable part in the history of New Zealand mountaineering".[3] By then Fyfe had established his reputation. In his later work Ross stated that in 1890 after a chance meeting on the Sealy Range, he made bold to give Fyfe his first lesson in mountaineering.

Ross and Fyfe soon gained the top of the range (there was no further mention of the dog). On such a day climbing can be exhilarating once limbs are loosened up. To Fyfe with his cycling background, the rhythmic movement, using the legs as economically as possible, would have been quite familiar. He certainly had the strength in his legs necessary to settle into a steady upward pace. As he climbed higher he would have felt the release of energy and the gradual adaptations, together with the minor discomforts. As the work gets harder, sweat begins to run down inside shirts, especially under the heat of a sun that becomes more intense the higher one climbs.

Gradually when the body adapts and the lungs meet the need for oxygen, it is possible to absorb some of the impressions of the surroundings that could previously not be appreciated. The vivid blue of the sky now may be better seen, together with the outrageous white glare of the sun reflected off the snow, contrasting with the varied browns of the rock strata. These images leave indelible memories in a highly sensitised consciousness. Such impressions, often recalled in detail later, are recorded almost automatically as one moves along seeking out the best route, seemingly in perpetual motion.

As Fyfe and Ross climbed higher the landscape opened and they consulted the map to identify points seen. Although Mt Sealy was a long way off, situated above the head of the Mueller and Metelille Glaciers, they decided to go on, obviously being fit enough to consider it worth making an attempt to reach it. They tried to keep to the top of the range, but progress slowed when what had been but a rock scramble steepened considerably. Here they halted and used Ross's binoculars to scan the side of the mountain ahead. To get around this barrier they descended about a thousand feet to the Mueller Glacier and then climbed back up again over an easy slope to a glacier that crowned the top of the range just below what they incorrectly thought was the final peak of Mt Sealy. Probably conscious of the need to hurry because of the time, they set off, clambering easily down over some looser rocks which eventually brought them onto a short snow slope. Ross made light of the difficulties, writing that although the ice was rather slippery they managed to cross

When additions were made to the Hermitage in 1890, the hole left from where the original building had been excavated was landscaped to form a lake.
Photo: Malcolm Ross

Access to the Tasman Glacier was made easier when this wire cage was put across the Hooker River. Fyfe used to retrieve the cage by climbing hand over hand along the wire rope.
Photo: Malcolm Ross

without the aid of ice axes. Some easy rock work followed this and then some exposed climbing, Ross using his alpenstock against the snow. Fyfe, not having an axe with him, preferred the safer footing afforded by rock.

It was thirsty work on such a blazing hot day, and they refreshed themselves by spreading handfuls of snow to melt on the warm brown rocks, letting the water trickle down into a hollow below. In this way they got a welcome drink. They then kept a direct course upwards, soon finding themselves on the edge of the glacier which they had seen lower down and which stretched upwards towards Mt Sealy for about three-quarters of a mile. Crossing this quite level glacier presented little difficulty and they easily rounded the next few crevasses.

29

In one place, with the heat of the day now intense, they again stopped to drink, finding icy water at a surface stream which ran for some distance over the ice and then down a crevasse. The temperature that is generated on a hot day on a high alpine plateau like the Annette can be intense, especially if there is not even a hint of a cool southerly wind. Ross and Fyfe now felt their skin starting to burn and their lips drying, and the glare reflecting off the snow made seeing very difficult. From time to time they sought out a comfortable spot for a rest on higher ground that was more open to the cooling breeze. Now much closer to the peak and keen to go as far as possible, they moved on at a quicker pace, occasionally stopping briefly to admire the view. Before them lay a panorama of mountains, all unclimbed peaks, and all possibly implanting an ambition in these young men to climb to their summits.

After some time they halted at the foot of a snow slope which blocked their progress. It was too steep to be climbed without steps being cut with an ice axe. Neither of them had brought an ice axe on the trip, Fyfe merely out on a walk and Ross not expecting to be doing any ice work. To the right they saw a narrow rock ridge which tapered off towards the Mueller Glacier at its lower end, but which ran right up to what appeared to be the final peak. They made directly for it. At first the ridge was steep, but it was composed of rock that gave good handholds and in time they gained the top of the arête. In one or two places it was so sharp that they almost crawled along on hands and knees, taking the utmost care. As they were not roped, a fall to either side would have been disastrous, because to right and left the rocks sloped away for hundreds of feet sheer down to the Metelille Glacier.

However, they toiled on upwards until 4.30 in the afternoon when they stopped on a sharp peak. Having gained a good vantage point (the description now points to its being not Mt Sealy but one of the smaller peaks in the region), they had a chance to rest. They gazed in wonder at the vast array of mountains stretched out in front of them. These are now contained in the Mt Cook National Park and are much climbed, but in 1890 it was still all virgin territory. To get to this point

View towards the névé of the Mueller Glacier, towards which Tom Fyfe and Malcolm Ross climbed on Fyfe's first visit in 1890.
Photo: Gavin Wills

they had been walking and climbing for over ten hours, and after admiring the view they decided to go no further; it was time to return to the hotel. After taking one last look around them, as climbers often do, etching lasting impressions in their minds, they turned their faces towards the Hermitage for the homeward journey.

Rather than descend the rock ridge which had taken them an hour to climb, they crossed a bergschrund and then glissaded down the steepish snow slope — sliding 300 feet in a few seconds. After glissading on the snow slopes above the Mueller and having a few difficulties choosing a route lower down the valley, by then in the gloom, they at last made their way back to the Hermitage, arriving about an hour after dark. Like many beginners who glissade, Fyfe had torn the seat out of his trousers, and during the rock-climbing he had opened up the sole of one of his boots.

What were Fyfe's reactions to his first experience of mountain climbing? His later achievements indicate that he was profoundly moved by it. On their first experience of an alpine area, whether as sightseers or climbers, people feel many different emotions: awe, fear, enchantment, curiosity, challenge and excitement. Scarcely anyone fails to respond with strong feelings in the presence of such enormous examples of the forces of nature. For some people intriguing questions are also likely to come to mind. Are those highest peaks climbable? Who has climbed them before? How would you do it? What would it feel like to get to the top?

It is highly likely that on that day in 1890 Tom Fyfe had some of those feelings and asked himself some of those questions. It seems that he enjoyed his introduction to the mountains and that he found Malcolm Ross's company pleasant.

In many ways they were contrasting figures. Ross, eight years older than Fyfe and a forthright man, was then private secretary to Sir James Mills, managing director of the Union Steamship Company in Dunedin. Formerly a journalist on the *Otago Daily Times* for eight years and later a parliamentary press correspondent in Wellington, Ross wrote two books and many newspaper articles about climbing.[4] Fyfe wrote well but seldom, and was more self-effacing. Their differing personalities did not keep them apart, however, and on several occasions in the next twenty years they joined up again, making an effective climbing pair.

1. J. Von Haast, *Geology of the Provinces of Canterbury and Westland, New Zealand,* (Christchurch: Times Office, 1879), p. 28.
2. M. Ross, *Aorangi,* (Wellington: Government Printer, 1892), p. 25.
3. M. Ross, *A Climber in New Zealand,* (London: Arnold, 1914), p. 49.
5. *Dictionary of New Zealand Biography* Vol. 2, (Wellington: Department of Internal Affairs, 1993), p. 119.

3

MT DE LA BECHE

Tom Fyfe's first experience of climbing began a long love affair with the mountains. Never again did competitive cycling hold the same attraction for him. Each working year he would save as much of his earnings as he could in order to spend time climbing at Mt Cook. In November 1892 he returned, keen to do as much climbing as possible. Although some of his time was spent on his own climbing trips, he was employed by Frank Huddleston and the Mt Cook Hermitage Company to assist with trips for the tourists to the glaciers and beyond. In this way he got to know other climbing enthusiasts.

There were few climbers, however, and there were still many problems in tackling the highest peaks. By modern standards, clothing and equipment were primitive — no light wind-proof clothing or sleeping bags, no convenient tents, no compact cooking gear or convenience foods, no flexible light-weight footwear, no crampons for ice or pitons for rock. (For some time after crampons had been developed and used in Europe, New Zealanders considered them not quite sporting.) Moreover there were virtually no shelters in alpine regions, nor any means of communication or rescue in emergencies. Enormous distances had to be travelled before darkness if a night out on the mountain was to be avoided. Routes would be tried and found to be too long, or they ran out into blank faces. Organisational problems appeared when parties were large, or if there were varying levels of skill within a group. There were no professionals to offer advice or instruction, and few books and contour maps were available. These pioneers were climbing in glacial areas that were virtually unexplored. In fact they were doing the exploring.

Gradually, however, especially between 1890 and 1895, much was learned. As one of a small band of vigorous colonial moun-taineers, Tom Fyfe had to teach himself how to climb, find out which routes offered the best possibility of success and learn how to minimise his chances of failure. Quite soon he became an audacious and innovative mountaineer, one that others were prepared to follow and whose critical decisions on advance or retreat they were prepared to accept. He spent enough time in the Mt Cook area to develop a good understanding of and respect for the vagaries and dangers of the weather systems which prevail there.

Fyfe's judgement about the weather accounts for some of his decisions to turn back just short of summits rather than risk a

Marmaduke Dixon, left, and Tom Fyfe in 1893, clothed and equipped for high climbing. On the leather straps over Dixon's shoulder was tied a swag containing clothing and food bound in an oilskin outer cloth. Ice axes were imported, but Fyfe later fashioned his own.
Source: Kinsey Collection, Canterbury Museum

34

night out and a change in the weather. Pioneer climbers had to rely entirely on observation and the readings of barometers. However, they were keenly aware of the effects of a nor'wester followed by a southerly change. Modern climbers, even with the advantage of long-range weather forecasting and scientific knowledge of cloud patterns to help them in the face of an impending weather change, can still make errors of judgment. Despite all the forecasts available today by radio to climbers in high huts, climbing in good weather can still be a chancy business, and nights out during climbs are carefully calculated to try to avoid bad weather.

These were the crucial factors which prevented early climbers having immediate success on what are today regarded as less difficult peaks. Early mountaineers recorded their frustrations and attempts because each climb seemed to advance useful knowledge. Each exploratory trip up the Mueller, Hooker, Tasman and Murchison Glaciers to the peaks beyond made a contribution to later climbers as well as giving personal satisfaction for the participants. But even access to the glacial valleys was difficult because of the dangerous rivers which had to be forded until wire cages on aerial ropeways were installed.

Fyfe and his contemporaries were determined and resilient, and they adapted quickly to the demands of the alpine regions. Arthur Harper cycled to the Hermitage from Christchurch, as he also did to the West Coast. George Mannering, in addition to his climbing exploits, took groups of friends on exploratory trips into the Arrowsmith Range. These adventurous young products of upper-class families believed they were re-kindling a pioneering spirit which was becoming lost among the gentry of Canterbury.

They were in a minority, however, and Harper deplored his fellow Christ's College old boys' lack of interest in the individual sports offering in the unexplored alpine areas on their doorsteps. In the early 1890s there were more than a hundred unclimbed mountains in the Mt Cook area. The only climb of significance since Green's attempt on Mt Cook had been Mannering and Dixon's near success by the same route in

December 1890. In the next twenty-four years there was much more mountaineering activity, but it was more than a decade after the First World War before the sport again attracted many people.

In 1892, as a guide for the Hermitage, Fyfe was leading excursions on to the Tasman Glacier and to the head of the Mueller Glacier. One of his trips was a crossing of Ball Pass, guiding Mr and Mrs Robert Fairbanks of New York in company with Jack Adamson. That climb, on 19 December 1892, was the first crossing of that pass by a woman.[1] Affording marvellous views of Mt Cook and the peaks in the Hooker Glacier area, this round trip became popular with tourists who wished to do a little more than just walk on the ice of the glaciers. By January 1893 Fyfe had been working as a guide on the glaciers for two months. There is nothing like a spell of glacier guiding to whet the appetite to climb higher, and he again joined company with Malcolm Ross, who with his wife, Forrest, was once more visiting the region, to attempt Mt De la Beche.

At that time its altitude was thought to be over 10,000 feet, which may account for the interest in it. It rises as a pyramid via a long mixed rock-and-snow ridge with tributary glaciers such as the Ranfurly cascading off its other ridges. Rearing up at the summit in a fine rock peak, it is certainly a summit worthy of attention. Just north of Mt De la Beche are two ice-clad pinnacles known as the Minarets, with a surveyed height of over 10,000 feet. The whole mass forms a substantial bulk, and compared with some of the other mountains in the region may have looked easier.

Today it is regarded as one of the less difficult mountains in the Mt Cook area. Before Fyfe's first effort there had been four unsuccessful attempts. Mannering, Dixon and Johnson reached an altitude of about 8,000 ft on 29 March 1889, but were not able to finish the route. On 11 March 1892 Harper and Hamilton made another attempt. Choosing a likely route up the Rudolf Glacier, they reached a point somewhere close to 9,000 ft. This bold effort was thwarted by Hamilton's becoming ill, and they returned at 6.30 pm, having been thirteen and a half

36

Mt De la Beche and
the Minarets above
the Tasman Glacier.
Photo: Colin Monteath.

hours on the climb. Four days later Harper was there again, this time accompanied by Jack Adamson of the Hermitage who was keen to have a break from his work. However, they were forced to give up at the same point Harper had reached before, driven back by a nor'wester so strong that on one occasion it blew them out of their steps. Not to be beaten easily, Harper and Adamson renewed the assault on the 19th, but after reaching the same point again, Harper's bad luck on the mountain struck once more when Adamson fell ill with severe stomach pains. Once again a descent had to be called before the summit had

37

been reached. Harper's determination to succeed had been defeated and he did not try again.

On 3 January 1893 Ross and Fyfe carried large swags up the Tasman Glacier and camped at the De la Beche bivouac. After raking up the gravel under the rock and making small indentations for their hips, they spread the tent and a blanket out as a mattress. The view from the bivouac is of Mts Meteor, Aigrette, Spencer and Jervois sitting airily above the massive contorted icefalls from which avalanches plunge daily to the glacier below. The broken nature of the area — 6,000 feet from the glacier to the peaks — ensures that even today most of these mountains have not been climbed from the Rudolf Glacier. It was a fine evening as Fyfe and Ross sat at the mouth of their cave watching the setting sun throw its pink canopy over the snow until it sank out of sight behind the bulk of Mt Haidinger.

But overnight the weather deteriorated. The small cavity under the bivouac which provides adequate shelter in fine weather was lashed by an invading storm. Successive groups of climbers had tried to keep the site dry by stacking up a wall of stones, but driving sleet and rain leaked through. In such conditions days spent waiting for the weather to improve can try one's patience. Fyfe and Ross brewed tea over the spirit lamp, breakfasted and then turned into bed again. There was little in the way of amusements except a copy of the *Sydney Bulletin* that Fyfe had put into his swag when leaving the Hermitage. After reading and then rereading everything in it, Ross mused that 'they were better off than a previous expedition whose only literature had been the labels on the meat tins'.[2]

At 5 am on the third day the weather had cleared enough for them to make hasty preparations for a climb of the mountain. They were soon moving quickly up the Rudolf Glacier, putting on the rope for protection when crevasses began to appear as they climbed higher. Not long afterwards, Ross recounted, 'Fyfe went through a hidden crevasse and found his legs dangling in space'. However, with Ross anchoring and keeping the rope taut, Fyfe was able to get himself out fairly quickly. Then with the kind of wry comment to Ross that was characteristic of him, he said, 'I've been wondering about what the sensation of falling into a crevasse would be like, as one of the guides told me that when he went through one that his heart was in his mouth; but now that I've experienced it I'm very disappointed. I felt no sensation at all. In fact I didn't have time to feel anything.'[3]

They continued to climb, keeping to the middle of the glacier where there were fewer crevasses and making for the western side of a rock ridge that descends from the shoulder of the peak. However, because of foggy weather that held on after the storm had abated, they had not been able to get a clear view up the ridge. When they did move onto the ridge they found that the first easy rocks quickly steepened into much more difficult climbing. In one particularly troublesome spot that fully tested Fyfe's ability, he had to assist Ross up with the use of the rope, 'somewhat amused', Ross recounted, 'from his safe position above'. Gradually the rock became almost perpendicular and they moved out onto snow slopes and had to begin cutting steps, as the snow had been hidden from the sun for several days and was too hard for their nailed boots to get a good enough grip. After climbing around avalanche debris rather than through it, fearing a recurrence, they eventually made their way back onto rock higher up the ridge, climbing a pinnacle of rock and hoping to get a view of the icefall.

Here at 12.30 pm they stopped and waited for twenty minutes, hoping for the weather to clear enough for them to continue. But as they waited, slowly at first and then more quickly, flakes of fine snow began to mingle with the mist. There was no point in continuing the climb and they reluctantly turned their backs on the mountain and began the descent. Emotions at such a turning point are usually mixed. There is disappointment at having expended so much energy without reaching the summit — perhaps not even having gained a good view. Naturally there is the doubt as to whether, if one had waited or proceeded further, there might have been a lucky clearance. There may perhaps be resignation, knowing that the best has not been good enough to conquer the mountain. When the time comes, it often comes abruptly: the die is cast.

Descending, they found that the steps they had cut, which should have helped them find their way, even in the mist, were now obliterated by the snow and the clouds. It was so difficult to see ahead that they kept close to the rocks and became disoriented for a while, but they climbed steadily downwards anyway. Eventually reaching easier slopes where they were sure of their ground in the snow, they began making exhilarating glissades. The advantages of saving time and effort by this breakneck method of descent have dangers as well as excitement — as Ross found out. He wrote: 'In one place, however, I came suddenly to grief, for while we were skimming down at a good pace, my foot went through the thin crust of snow, and I found myself suddenly tripped up in a crevasse and shot down the slope head foremost in the direction of some bergschrunds. A yell to Fyfe who was on the rope following me, however, soon put matters right, for, quick as lightning, driving his axe deep into the snow, he anchored himself and I found my downwards progress arrested as suddenly as it had commenced.'[4]

Left to right: Jack Adamson, Minnie Mannering, George Mannering, Tom Fyfe, date unknown.
Source: Kinsey Collection, Canterbury Museum

The strength of Fyfe's arms and his quick reflexes — the hall-mark of a good climber — prevented further mishap, including the possibility of both climbers ending up in the crevasse. Despite the risks of leg injuries, Ross and Fyfe had a penchant for glissading at every possible opportunity. It certainly enabled them to make a quick descent in this instance and they were soon back at the bivouac. They changed out of their wet clothes and prepared a meal for the evening before indulging their passion for photography out on the glacier later in the afternoon.

The next day, their food stocks running low and the mountain still unclimbed, they decided to go down the glacier to Ball Hut for fresh supplies. If the weather had improved by then, they would redouble their efforts. The trip down with little gear was quickly accomplished, and on the way they met Adamson coming up the glacier with two clients who wanted to see the upper parts of the glacier. As the weather was clearing, it was decided that the two parties would join up and that Adamson would join Ross and Fyfe for another attempt on De la Beche the next day. With the new arrangements made, Fyfe volunteered to carry on to the Hermitage to tell Frank Huddleston and Forrest Ross what was proposed and then return to De la Beche bivouac the same evening, ready to climb the next morning. Fyfe clearly enjoyed moving around the area on his own. He was also prepared to push himself to extreme physical efforts, and as Ross wrote, he 'gaily set about his self-imposed trip'. When the remainder of the party arrived at the bivouac early in the evening they were very surprised to see him close behind, hard on their heels only half a mile away.

In one day he had covered forty miles over ice and rough ground on foot and on horseback. From De la Beche to Ball Hut he had taken 2 hours 55 minutes; from Ball Hut to the Hermitage on horseback 2 hours 17 minutes; the return journey of fourteen miles from the Hermitage to Ball Hut had taken 2 hours 20 minutes, and from Ball Hut back to the De la Beche bivouac, 2 hours 10 minutes. Actually quicker on foot than on horseback, he had run most of the fourteen miles so that he could find his way through the crevasses at De la Beche corner before night-fall.[6] This extraordinary capacity to move quickly over rough

Climbers return from the Malte Brun Range across the Tasman Glacier to De la Beche bivouac after collecting scrubwood for their evening fire — a round trip of three to four hours.
Source: Canterbury Museum

country characterised many of his climbs. On this occasion, however, he had overdone it, as he was to find out to his regret next day.

Mountain mornings can hold a rare beauty, a beauty born of silence. Glacial streams which flow freely during the day lie frozen, potential avalanches remain held in place by lower temperatures, rocky moraine adheres to the glacial ice, and the last vestiges of night add to the tranquillity. Climbers can feel intrusive on such a scene as they plod along. Eyes strain to see where to put the next footstep; sometimes a stumble occurs, making foreign grating sounds with the clatter of boots and equipment. Conversation is normally at a minimum, as limbs loosen up and stomachs digest the midnight breakfast. Hopes abound that the weather will hold fine, that good views will be seen and summits achieved, and that everybody will manage to stay on the mountain for the rest of the day. After the plod up the glacier, the steeper climbing begins and thoughts change. Will the snow turn into ice? Will the rock be loose or sound? Is everything right with the gear? Sunrise is a happy occasion: lights can be put away and a good look taken at the intended route up the mountain. The feeling at this time is often: 'Let's get cracking'.

It was a frosty morning as Tom Fyfe, Malcolm Ross, Jack Adamson and his client Gibbs, after a late start, began the sixth attempt to climb Mt De la Beche. They made good time up the Rudolf Glacier, pausing at intervals to admire the rose-tinted peaks as the sun came up. When they had climbed onto the mountain via its western approaches at a point just below the icefall on the glacier, Adamson started cutting steps. As ice chips smashed down and rapid progress was made, they felt confident they would make the peak by about one o'clock. Higher up the mountain, however, they once again had difficulty picking out a route.

On reaching a long snowy plateau they were confronted with a steep snow slope leading up to a saddle between De la Beche and the lower of the Minarets. To the right was another slope leading to the rocks that Harper had climbed to, and these seemed to lead onto the main ridge and thence to the peak. They discussed the best route, and when Jack Adamson's opinion won the day, the whole party moved towards the rock route away from further step cutting, because this had begun to slow the party down. Adamson, who had led admirably for an hour and a half and had cut over 500 steps, needed a rest, Ross had soon found his hands blistered from the work, and Fyfe was beginning to feel the strain of his forty-mile trip only twelve hours before. Gibbs, a complete novice, had come primarily to botanise, and was incapable of doing anything other than follow the others. Despite these problems, they soon gained the crest of the ridge and the peak was now tantalisingly close.

To their profound disappointment they found that the ridge stopped abruptly and a great gap existed between their end of the ridge and the summit of the mountain. Fyfe felt he had gone far enough, and Adamson thought the route too difficult to continue. With more time and energy in reserve, they might well have been able to retrace their steps and try a different approach but after a general discussion all reluctantly agreed they could go no further. After some photography they began the descent, following their line of steps, cutting new ones where necessary and glissading down slopes that seemed to have a clear passage. After a long day on the mountain they arrived back at the bivouac late in the evening. That had been the highest point reached by any of these men at that time in their climbing careers. The next day they moved off, tramping the twenty miles down to the Hermitage where they enjoyed hot baths.

They had been thwarted in the attempt on De la Beche, but they had also benefited from the experience. They had learned about the effect of sunburn from the glare on a hot day and the discomfort of snowblindness. They had spent a lot of time finding routes and becoming familiar with the pros and cons of climbing on snow or on rock. They learned that top physical condition was required for success. They had doubt-less also learned that speed plays a large part in determining whether a climb is completed: the amount of step cutting necessary to get to over 9,000 feet had been time-consuming. The effort that Tom Fyfe had expended the day before had exhausted him, and Jack Adamson had shouldered the major workload of the day. It must have been disappointing for Adamson to have failed at his third attempt. But in the end it was the vast gap in the ridge that defeated them, and they could not have known about that.

Valuable lessons can be learnt from failures, and the mountain-eering literature contains many accounts of unsuccessful at-tempts made on peaks as well as detailing successes. To some extent, climbing techniques are governed by equipment. Where possible, climbers of last century climbed on rock if the snow was too hard to kick or cut into steps. If the rock was so difficult that steps had to be cut in ice or snow, then progress was slowed. The rope was usually kept on so that falls could be arrested by companions taking a bight of rope around the shaft of an ice axe plunged into the snow. This technique, called the New Zealand belay, was quite effective in snow. But it was less so on ice because companions had to stand in the steps that had been cut and do their very best not to slip. As a last resort, if someone did slip, the pick end of the axe was thrust into the ice.

Fyfe began to link sustained and steep rock climbing with short bursts of step cutting in snow and ice. This enabled him to climb higher and further in a shorter time than his fellow mountaineers. For descending snow slopes, he was keen on glissading — skidding down in a sitting position as if skiing, and using his ice axe as a brake behind him to slow his speed. Good balance and steady nerves were essential, because if one came upon steep ice during the glissade the chances of being able to arrest the downward plunge were remote.

Fyfe tried to learn from every climb, and he gradually developed the confidence and the skills that gave him an extremely high level of competence. His enthusiasm and skill was soon to be complemented in the person of George Graham who arrived to work at the Hermitage during the next climbing season. He proved to be a redoubtable and entertaining climbing partner.

1. Unsourced newspaper article in the scrapbook of A.P. Harper. Hocken Library.
2. M. Ross, "On De La Beche — The Chronicle of a Failure," *New Zealand Alpine Journal (NZAJ)* Vol. 1, No. 3, (April 1893): 125-133, & Vol. 1, No. 4, (November 1893): 179-190.
3. *Ibid.*
4. *Ibid.*

4

FIRST ATTEMPT ON MOUNT COOK

Now in his early twenties, Fyfe was becoming a formidable climber. Five feet eight inches tall and weighing thirteen stone, he was solidly built, and his unusual ability on both rock and ice had already been noticed. His reputation began to spread amongst the small climbing community which had formed in Canterbury and Otago. By 1893, having completed his plumbing apprenticeship and become relatively independent, he had more time to devote to alpine interests. He also began to read the literature on mountaineering .

Living in Timaru meant that he was ideally placed to travel to the Hermitage. The Mt Cook Company directors were based in Timaru, and because Fyfe lived nearby and now knew the alpine area well, they often employed him. During the 1893-94 climbing season lasting from November to March he lived almost continuously at Mt Cook and thus had more time than other mountaineers to wait for good weather to attempt climbs. During the winter periods between climbing seasons his work helped to keep him fit, so when he travelled up to the Hermitage to climb he was in good physical shape.

Winter nights in Timaru also provided time to read. Literature on technical aspects of mountaineering was arriving from England and being passed around the climbing community. The main books in circulation at the time were those by Claude Dent and Claude Wilson, illustrated by J.G. Willink and Ellis Carr. Fyfe probably read the most popular book on mountaineering, *The Badminton Library,* very keenly. The advice in such books formed the basis on which New Zealand climbers developed, supported by actual experience in the mountains, learning about weather and snow conditions and about the dangers of spending a night out on a mountain.

Essential climbing equipment which could not be made in New

This English advertisement from the 1890s shows some equipment which was not used in New Zealand at the time — notably ice axes with removeable heads, and screw-in spikes for ice climbing. The compressed leather studs shown are likely to have been used by Jack Clark when he climbed Mt Tasman in February 1895 with Edward Fitzgerald and Mattias Zurbriggen — who used crampons.
Source: Canterbury Museum.

Zealand had to be imported, usually from England. Alpine climbing was one of the grandest sports of the Victorian era, and from the 1860s many young English climbers from among the wealthy classes went to Switzerland to climb the great peaks there. Several shops in London catered to their needs. Reputable suppliers, such as Hill and Son in the Haymarket, would provide a standard ice axe, with a case for its head and a wrist sling, for £2 2s 6d. They could even supply ice axes with movable heads. Rope made of the best hemp that could be found and a rucksack could be purchased for £1 3s. For better purchase on ice there were studs manufactured from compressed leather which could be screwed into the soles of boots. Climbers completed their personal gear with goggles, an aneroid, a water bottle and a folding lantern.[1]

At no little expense Tom Fyfe bought the bare essentials — an ice axe and a climbing rope of the best quality. He improvised a good deal, however, becoming adept at doing so because of the experience of climbing from tent camps. When fuel ran low, for example, they would boil a pannikin of drink over a lighted candle put through a hole in the base of an empty food can, with

47

fine wire mesh on the top of the can to hold the pannikin. To keep warm Fyfe would often light a candle under his blanket.

In the early 1890s there were enough mountaineers for them to have mutual interests and to think of forming a club — one to which climbers and explorers could belong. Impetus came from Arthur Harper of Christchurch who had climbed in Europe and was already a member of the Alpine Club in London. People began to realise that with the passage of time knowledge of some of the early exploration work in this country was being lost. Nothing was being published that covered work done in New Zealand's vast mountain-scape. On 11 March 1891 George Mannering and Arthur Harper called a meeting to discuss the founding of a club. Harper became the driving force, and officers and committee members were elected at a meeting held on 28 July 1891.

The first annual general meeting of the New Zealand Alpine Club was later convened at Mortons Hotel in Sumner on 22 November 1892. It was open to members of both sexes and by 1892 it counted among its thirty-five members and nine sub-scribers most of the people who had contributed to the explora-tion of New Zealand's mountain areas in recent years. When Tom Fyfe joined the club in 1894 he was its fifty-first member.[2] For a small country with few traditions of alpine climbing, these numbers compared well with a membership of approximately 450 in the London counterpart. The New Zealand Alpine Club's annual membership fee was set at a guinea (£1 1s), a consider-able commitment at a time when a week's wages might amount to little more than that. Among the club's members Tom Fyfe could count many of his friends and climbing acquaintances, including Malcolm Ross, Kenneth Ross, Marmaduke Dixon and George Mannering.

Although he did not reach any high summits in New Zealand, George Mannering helped to get mountaineering accepted as a sport in this country. Born in 1862 in Oxford, Canterbury, he carried out extensive exploration of glaciers and alpine passes besides making several attempts to climb Mt Cook. He also explored the Murchison Glacier, the first to do so. In February

1892 he visited the Godley Glacier in company with Malcolm Lean and a shepherd, James Annan, who accompanied him on many of his journeys. They climbed the Godley Glacier from its terminal moraine to the Sealy Pass at 5,800 feet, crossing that pass for the first time and descending into Scone Creek on the West Coast side of the Main Divide. Here they had a serious accident when Lean fell between eighty and one hundred feet at the terminal face. He suffered a dislocated shoulder and was badly cut, so they returned back over the pass instead of completing the journey to the West Coast. In May 1893 Mannering together with Lean and C. H. Inglis of Timaru made an attempt to climb Mt Arrowsmith in the upper Rakaia region. In trying to climb the peak they had difficulties finding a route and found themselves on a high saddle at 7,400 feet on a subsidiary ridge between the Cameron and Douglas Glaciers. Here the ice was immensely hard, and step cutting slowed the party to the point where they could go no further. A nineteen-hour day saw them return to Lake Heron after dark.

Marmaduke Dixon farmed at West Eyreton, and although according to Mannering he possessed limited natural climbing ability, he made frequent trips to the Canterbury ranges.[3] His first alpine trip to the Mt Cook region had been in 1887 with Mannering and Inglis when he attempted to climb the Haast Ridge with a view to climbing Mt Cook. On that occasion they were beaten back by soft snow and rain. Dixon was a man of large physical stature and he had great endurance. His skill with horses was exemplified in March 1889 when he drove a tandem team 500 miles from his farm to Mt Cook and back. Possessing tremendous energy and enthusiasm, Dixon enjoyed a challenge and was highly competitive. He once broached to his canoeing and climbing friend, George Park, the idea of a race down the Waimakariri River in canoes. Although Park was a strong canoeist and swimmer, he declined Dixon's invitation — perhaps wisely. However, by 1893 Marmaduke Dixon was thirty-one years of age. For him and his old schoolmate George Mannering their earliest mountaineering days were now some years in the past — yet they had still not climbed Mt Cook.

They now happened to link up with Tom Fyfe, then emerging

Notice of the first annual general meeting of the New Zealand Alpine Club, 1892. The club provided a venue for members to share their alpine experiences and a journal which, in text and photographs, recorded members' achievements.
Source: Hocken Library

49

Marmaduke Dixon,
left, and Tom Fyfe
on the Grand
Plateau in 1893.
This is the first
recorded use of skis
in New Zealand.
These ones, made
by Dixon from
reaper blades, were
difficult to control
but were helpful in
crossing soft snow.
Dixon's shirt and
waistcoat shows his
response to the heat
reflected off the
snow — as do the
snowglasses of both
climbers. Fyfe
carries a second
rope in case it is
needed.
Photo: G.E. Mannering,
Kinsey Collection,
Canterbury Museum

as their most likely competitor for that honour. Dixon and
Mannering had envisaged a larger party than this, one which
included A. M. Ollivier, Malcolm Lean and C.H. Ensor, but
these latter three withdrew for various reasons. This left only
Mannering and Dixon for the attempt. Fyfe had left Timaru
early in November 1893 to work and climb at Mt Cook, and in
that month he became involved for the first time with Dixon's
attempts on Mt Cook. Dixon wrote thus about the inclusion of
Fyfe: 'We arrived at the Hermitage as usual in heavy rain. Here
Mr and Mrs Adamson are in charge on behalf of the Hermitage
Company but one sadly misses Mr Huddleston in the capacity
of "entertaining host", which is his forte. At the Hermitage we
are pleased to find Mr Fyfe who with Mr Adamson has just
returned from making a cache of provisions to climb Mt De la

Beche. Fyfe whose spirit of adventure is as keen as the mountain air agrees to accompany us to the top of Mt Cook if we get there.'[4] Fyfe had to pay a price for joining the party, however — a stipulation of which Dixon later wrote: 'The party was reduced to Mannering and myself again, and by this time we came to consider we had a sort of special interest in that peak, and consequently when I fell in with Tom Fyfe, we made the compact that if we failed after trying together, he was not to climb Mt Cook by Green's route for two years, excepting Mannering and I were in the party.'[5]

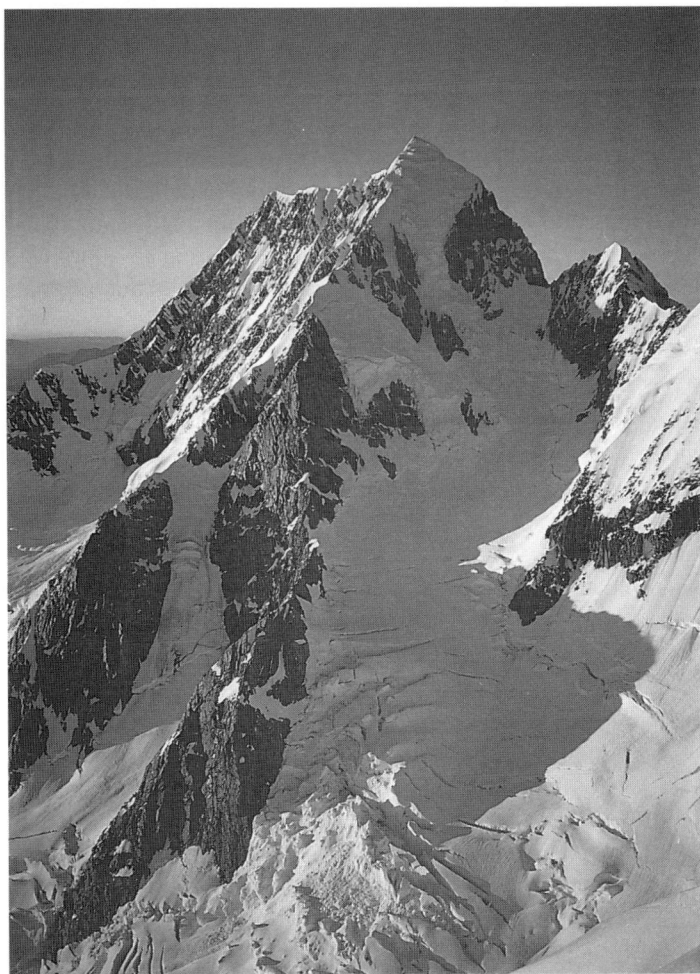

The northern approaches to Mt Cook: Zurbriggen Ridge, centre left, Linda Glacier, centre, North Ridge, right, Bowie Ridge. foreground.
Photo: Chris Curry, Hedgehog House

51

Plans for an attempt were agreed, and Fyfe and Dixon duly set out for Ball Hut along the track which had recently been constructed by the government to encourage visitors to the area. There was still a large amount of snow in the region. Their reasons for attempting the peak so early in the season are not clear; possibly they thought that the crevasses in the Linda Glacier would be more easily negotiated because they would be covered with snow. In 1890 both Dixon and Mannering had had difficulties with crevasses. Perhaps of greater significance was that Marmaduke Dixon knew that Malcolm Ross also planned to attempt Mt Cook that summer, but Ross was not a party to the agreement. Whatever the reason for the early start, Dixon was well prepared, having made two pairs of skis from reaper blades on his farm. Mannering knew them as Norwegian snow shoes. This was the first use of skis in New Zealand for any purpose in the mountains. Dixon believed they would be useful in crossing the soft snow of the Grand Plateau, thereby gaining valuable time and conserving energy for the long climb to the summit. He later wrote that he had considered the use of such equipment even before reading Captain Nansen's book about crossing Greenland.

After reaching Ball Hut, Dixon and Fyfe were to climb up the Haast Ridge and establish a camp and then return to Ball Hut to meet Mannering whose sister, Mrs Westland, was to accompany him to that point. Brodrick had chosen the site of Green's fifth camp as the safest place for the hut because it was protected from avalanches by the spur above it. The main concern was soakage from the Ball Glacier forming a lake between the moraine and the hill. This shows just how high the Ball Glacier was then: today it is three to four hundred feet below the moraine wall. The hut was then a small building, only nineteen feet long and twelve feet wide, divided into two compartments; each compartment had four bunks in it, a large tin-lined box for blankets and a table. The exterior was clad in corrugated iron and lined with Willesden roofing paper. With an earthen floor and all cooking done outside over stoves made from tins, it gave rudimentary and yet quite adequate shelter. The Ball Glacier was sometimes used as a natural refrigerator with sides of mutton being stored in the ice. The actual job of getting

building materials to the site had been a tedious one, most of the pieces having been carried up. Only the short pieces could be packed on packhorses which themselves found it difficult; the one carrying the long iron, for instance, was completely covered except for its legs, the poor brute having to keep its head in one position all the time — no mean feat over difficult country.

On the Haast Ridge in 1893 Tom Fyfe, left, and Marmaduke Dixon use the scant shelter provided by a large rock overhanging the bivouac platform. Photo: G.E. Mannering, 1893.

The bivouac that Fyfe and Dixon stocked on the Haast Ridge was at 7,000 feet. This was Fyfe's first visit to the Grand Plateau and doubtless he would have been impressed by the panoramic view from the camp of all the peaks of the Tasman area and across to the Malte Brun Range. They stayed there overnight. Describing the scene, Dixon wrote, 'It is a strange place to pass a night — this bivouac, a great overhanging stone about 10 feet high and over-hung some three feet six inches with a little flat place six feet square at its base, around which we have erected a little rampart of stones some 15 inches high.' They did not bother to use a tent, relying on the shelter and their own judgements about the weather.

53

Mannering meanwhile become concerned for their safety. There had been some confusion about when Dixon and Fyfe would return to Ball Hut, and he expected them twenty-four hours earlier. When they did not appear he set out to look for them. He said he eventually sat down on a rock wondering if he was looking for live men or not. However, his worst fears were soon dispelled. 'After an hour's continual waiting, the monotony of which was varied by more shouting on my part, I suddenly heard a faint reply far far below, and, making for the nearest couloir, went down with a mild avalanche and came across Dixon and Fyfe, as merry as sandboys, and anything but mangled corpses. If I had possessed a gun I should have shot them on the spot.'[6] With the confusion resolved, they all returned to Ball Hut where the industrious Dixon manufactured an extra pair of skis out of an old packing case.

Next day in fine November weather they left for the Haast bivouac, waking at midnight to a frosty moonlit scene. A quick climb took them up the remaining rock to the plateau above. Here they picked up the skis which Dixon and Fyfe had left there two days previously. With such an early start in fine conditions and with skis to assist them, they must have felt at this point that their venture had a good chance of success. Fyfe carried a camera with him, as did Mannering, and when they put their skis on there was time for some photography, the first on the Grand Plateau. They photographed the full vista with panoramic shots. Describing the scene before them, Mannering wrote, 'It was now 4 am. Before us, as we faced towards the Linda Glacier (SW), rose up what I suppose is one of the most magnificent scenes of mountain glory in the New Zealand Alps. The rocky mass of Aorangi, clothed here and there with enormous rooflike glacier, rose in stupendous grandeur, presenting a face of unparalleled magnificence. A little to our right hoary Tasman stood out boldly, glistening in the morning sunlight, and beginning to shed his daily avalanche onto the plateau. Behind us, a little to our left, we could look around and see the maze of crevasses which appears at the top of the Hochstetter Icefall, above which we now were, and away beyond this the peaks of the Malte Brun

Getting skis ready to use on the Grand Plateau in an attempt to climb Mt Cook in November 1893.
Photo: G.E. Mannering

and Liebig ranges, and further still the bold rocky mass of Mt Jukes appeared against a glorious crimson sunrise.'[7]

They made good progress across the plateau, finding they did not need to use the skis as they could walk on the hard frosted surface without breaking through. However, having in mind that once the sun was on the snow in the morning it would quickly soften and make the return journey tiresome, they made the skis into a sledge and put them on the end of the rope trailing behind. By 5 am they had reached the rocks where the Linda Glacier meets the plateau and they began climbing up the the glacier in a maze of crevasses. To make any progress at all required judicious route finding. Beginning a series of traverses from one side of the glacier to the other, they moved up what quickly became a difficult route.

Green had climbed this way in 1882 and Mannering and Dixon had used the same approach in 1890. By 1892 it had changed greatly, possibly because of unusually heavy snowfalls in previous winters. Now faced with gigantic blocks of ice and many crevasses deep enough to take a house, their resolve to complete the route began to weaken. While both Fyfe and Dixon were going well, Mannering was faltering — not surprising as he had come straight from his job in the Christchurch branch of the Union Bank of Australia. They kept plugging steps, but they were all starting to feel the effects of the heat now being focused on the Linda Glacier, and they began to suffer from snow-burn on their hands and faces. The heat sapped their energy, and with no significant protection they found it hard to keep going. Prolonged exposure to the ultraviolet rays reflected back off the snow can lead to second-degree burns. By 8 am they were still 3,000 feet below the summit, having reached the point where the glacier takes a leftward direction. Here they were forced to make a decision. Above, they could see that the route was heavily broken up with giant seracs — some of them 250 feet high, in Dixon's estimate — and there were many crevasses. Despite the intense heat they had to keep covered up in their tweed coats, while behind them the numerous snow bridges over which they had crawled on the ascent would be melting fast. There was also the constant threat of the avalanches that could engulf them at any moment, falling, as they irregularly do, across this route.

Well beaten by the conditions, they began the descent. Tom Fyfe wrote that the decision to turn back was 'because of the soft snow'. He was never convinced that this was route by which he would prefer to climb Mt Cook, if only because of the ever-present danger of avalanches. The problems with crevasses could also be heart-stopping as climbers wriggled their way across gaping caverns trusting to sometimes frail snow-bridges. At one point as the party began the descent two of them ended up dangling in different crevasses at the same time, held only by the rope between them. Eventually, however, they reached their skis and made good use of them in crossing the now soft snow of the Grand Plateau. At the top of the Haast Ridge they dispensed with the skis, leaving them there for future use, and descending to the Tasman Glacier they returned to Ball Hut.

Mannering retained an active interest in mountaineering, contributing to journals and later being elected a life member of the Alpine Club in London. He never lost his love of climbing, and in 1921 spent six weeks in Switzerland climbing in Chamonix, Zermatt and Grindalwald, conquering the Matterhorn at the age of sixty — an achievement indicative of his ability and determi-

A crevasse on the Linda Glacier, and in the foreground a snowbridge across it. Before attempting to cross snowbridges, climbers had to test each one to see whether it would bear a person's weight. Although he led several parties across the Linda in attempts on Mt Cook, Fyfe regarded the route as dangerous.
Source: Canterbury Museum

nation. Marmaduke Dixon had temporarily to console himself about the failure on Mt Cook with the thought that 'the summit of that hillock has been untrodden by man for perhaps a million or two years and why should we expect to be the first'.[8] The defeat merely strengthened his determination to climb the mountain by the same route.

For Tom Fyfe the attempt furthered his knowledge of the areas on that side of Mt Cook, but it may also have set him thinking about alternative routes to the summit. He then began a long summer of climbing. In the 1893-94 season he was in the mountains almost continuously for five months, mainly as an amateur but on other occasions working as a guide for the Mt Cook Hermitage Company. From camps low in the glacial valleys he climbed with speed, endurance and skill, attaining the first really high summits and setting standards for New Zealand mountaineering. A few months later Marmaduke Dixon, as secretary of the New Zealand Alpine Club, wrote of him thus: 'That summer Fyfe came out in brilliant colours, and I think proved that New Zealand can produce men capable of

Tom Fyfe, left, is belaying Marmaduke Dixon across a crevasse-prone part of the Grand Plateau. With a sugar-bag rucksack on his back, Dixon is crawling so as to distribute his weight more evenly. The photographer was George Mannering, the third member of this party attempting to climb Mt Cook in November 1893.

Photo by G.E. Mannering, in Kinsey Collection, Canterbury Museum

58

Jack Adamson, left, and Tom Fyfe assess the rock climbing on the newly opened Wakefield Track. The looseness of the rock in the Mt Cook region was a problem for climbers because handholds could give way unexpectedly.
Source: Kinsey Album, Alexander Turnbull Library

any reasonable Alpine feat.'[9] From 1890 until 1894 Tom Fyfe was a member or the leader of every party that set out to climb Mt Cook.

59

1   Hill and Sons (London) advertisement for climbing equipment. Canterbury Museum.
2. Record of qualifications of members on election to New Zealand Alpine Club 1891. Hocken Library.
3. G. E. Mannering, "Memories of Marmaduke John Dixon," *NZAJ* Vol. 3, No. 12, (December 1922): 123-130.
4. M. J. Dixon, "The Siege of Mt Cook," *NZAJ* Vol. 1, No. 5, (May 1894): 245-258.
5   M. J. Dixon, "The Attempts on Aorangi from the Eastern Side," *NZAJ* Vol. 2, No. 7, (May 1895): 5-19..
6.   G. E. Mannering, *Alpine Journal (London)* (August 1894): 10.
7. *Ibid.*
8. Dixon, May 1894.
9. Dixon, May 1895.

5

ON THE FOOTSTOOL

The Mt Cook region can be beset by long periods of rough weather, but for visitors the first clear view is breathtaking. North from the Hermitage the South Face of Mt Cook rears up, unmistakably. From there the Main Divide stretches left, back towards the viewer, marked in turn by Mt Hicks, a high fluted dome of rock and ice, Mt La Perouse, a large square bulky peak, then a line of peaks of lower altitude until, directly to the west, The Footstool and Mt Sefton with its tapestry of icefields loom

On the Main Divide close to the Hermitage stands The Footstool, which Tom Fyfe and George Graham approached via the East Ridge on the right of this photograph.
Photo: Colin Monteath, Hedgehog House

George Graham, from Waimate, unrelated to the West Coast Grahams. A protégé of Tom Fyfe.
Source: *South Canterbury: a record of settlement.*

up to dominate the view. The eye is attracted not only by these two high rocky summits but also by the enormous web-like entanglement of the Huddleston Glacier which hangs precipitously on the mountainside as if suspended there. The thunderous reports of avalanches hurtling towards the valley floor are an everyday sound, their billowing clouds of airborne snow and ice easily seen from the Hermitage area.

Accessible from the Hermitage, The Footstool is an attractive pyramidal peak. For Fyfe it also offered the possibility of seeing the upper western slopes of Mt Cook rising from the Hooker Glacier. He had already reconnoitred the possible approaches to it, spending his spare time climbing alone up to the snow line on the nearby peaks. From the Hermitage The Footstool looks to be an integral part of Mt Sefton. However, from its summit it can be seen that it is separated from that fortressed mountain by a long, knife-like and tortuous ridge. Further high ridges radiate off the mountain to the north, east and south, giving it a complexity so that the mountain stands as a distinctive peak in its own right. From the summit, Mt Sefton's East Ridge descending to Tuckett Col seems and enormous distance away. (The long ridge between Mt Sefton and The Footstool remained untrodden until the early 1960s when two Auckland climbers, Jim Sheffield and Peter Miller, boldly climbed in both directions and included an ascent of Mt Sefton en route.)

Tom Fyfe was doubtless attracted to The Footstool both as a mountaineering objective — a virgin peak — and as a viewpoint. It formed the perfect stance from which to scan the Main Divide for a pass that could link the West Coast with the Hermitage. The mountain is 9073 feet high and has several fine hanging glaciers and crenellated rock ridges, the East Ridge being the most prominent feature visible from the Hermitage area. Although from a distance the clarity and fine line of this ridge has an appeal, it is not until climbers are on it that they are aware of the extreme instability of the rock — a feature of New Zealand's central alps. Large rocks with little holding them together sit precariously on top of one another. On such rock, mountaineers test each hold they use and trust that not all their holds will come away at the same time. The final peak rises in a triangular shape with steep drops to the east and west. The climb from the floor of the Hooker valley, very demanding in terms of vertical height, requires a long day in the mountains.

During the summer of 1893-94 Tom Fyfe met George Graham who had arrived to work at the Hermitage as a maintenance carpenter and general hand and also assisting parties and packing in supplies.[1] A year older than Fyfe, Graham was born in Waimate. His Irish father had emigrated to New Zealand in 1867 and was for twenty years the clerk of the magistrates' court in Waimate. After the death of his mother when he was quite young, George was brought up by the local school teacher, Mr Bannerman, and his wife, who were childless. His education was completed at primary school and he became a qualified carpenter. Solidly built, his strength and fitness was augmented by working as a musterer in the Lake Te Anau district and then sheep stations in the Mackenzie basin.

Fyfe and Graham became a very effective climbing team. Their physical similarities enabled them to move at maximum speed on several long climbs from low levels. Not encumbered with others of lesser standard who might slow their progress, they now set out to tackle a series of virgin peaks, beginning with The Footstool.

On 19 January 1894 a heavy blanket of snow fell in the region making conditions unsuitable. Not until 29 January had enough snow melted from the rock ridges for Graham and Fyfe to consider an ascent. Fyfe believed that to have a good chance of success they would need to travel on rock as much as possible, rather than endure the slow process of step cutting on snow. For this reason they decided to climb in the general direction of the rocky East Ridge. On the evening of 30 January they readied themselves to make the climb on the next day, as their available time was limited. After the customary packing of essential climbing gear in the evening they planned for an early start. Following an unceremonious awakening by Jack Adamson at 2.30 am for breakfast, in preparation for the day's exertions they ate everything on the table, and, Fyfe says, 'asked for more'.[2]

In the 1890s a swing bridge replaced the wire cage over the Hooker River, an improvement that was much appreciated by climbers. Here, it is being used to drive sheep to graze on the Wakefield Spur.
Source: Canterbury Museum

Well fed, they left the snugness of the Hermitage in the dark and moved quickly over the track which had recently been formed. Their eyes quickly adjusted to the slightest change in light. When the first glimmer of daylight appeared in the sky they were able to pick their way across the terminal moraine of the Mueller Glacier to the foot of a leading spur which falls from the mountain, its base a mixture of tussock, soil and broken rock. Fyfe's reconnoitres were paying off: he had not only climbed on these lower slopes, he had also been on Mt Wakefield on the opposite side of the Hooker valley to see what the best approach might be on the upper slopes of The Footstool. Confident that they were on a good route, they forged ahead. Fyfe wrote: 'Striking up the bed of the mountain torrent that issues from the Tewaewe, the water-worn rocks gave splendid footing. We then skirted up the spur, with the Tewaewe on our immediate left. The climb from the "snout" of the Tewaewe to the first snow slope is very steep, mostly over bad but climbable rock.'[3] They quickly reached the prominent dome-shaped ridge where the Sefton bivvy is now situated.

64

The view from this point is wonderful. To the north Mt Cook dominates the head of the Hooker valley; to the south lies the amazing entanglement of hanging glaciers that fall for thousands of feet from the summit of Mt Sefton. High above them The Footstool awaited their approach. They recommenced climbing unroped because of the easy angle, but soon found that the going alternated between soft snow and harder conditions.

The East Ridge is renowned for the looseness of its rock; such is its fragility that the slightest touch can send down a fusillade of boulders upon unsuspecting climbers. From a distance its appearance is deceiving: it seems to be a strong line of rock likely to provide a straightforward yet steep climb. Writing of the condition of the ridge, Fyfe said: 'This rock on near approach, we found to be very rotten, crumbling away at the slightest touch. We could not climb without dislodging rocks, and had to keep as close to each other as possible. Fairly good progress was made for another half hour, but the higher we got the worse the rock became, until at last we had to move with the utmost caution.'[4]

Eventually they reached a very difficult section where the shattered ridge reared up with steep drops on either side. The risk of falling because of loose rock was high: holds were likely to give way as soon as any weight was placed on them. While climbing up to this point Fyfe had noticed that there were alternative routes which led off to the right, down toward the Eugenie Glacier, and these now looked more inviting than the prospect ahead. They decided to descend to the glacier below, thereby losing 700 feet of hard-won gains. However, having done so they began to make better progress.

It was turning into an eventful climb, and for George Graham a testing introduction to mountaineering. They were continually bombarded with rocks falling from the ridge above and they had to cross delicate snowbridges on the glacier by wriggling over them lying on their stomachs. Graham could have been forgiven if he had thoughts about the sanity of the undertaking. Any such misgivings would probably have been increased by the unfortunate loss of the rucksack containing their food when the straps loosened and let the day's provisions spill out, cascade down the glacier and finally drop into a crevasse. With that loss and some route-finding difficulties, they must have been sorely tempted to resign themselves to defeat on this occasion. Fyfe described some of these problems they encountered: 'After advancing a short way, the glacier became so broken that we were compelled to keep right against the arête, from which stones were falling continuously. In fact during the whole of the ascent our greatest trouble was the falling of stones. The fall of snow, followed by a sudden thaw, was no doubt accountable for this. After some step cutting, the end of the snow slope we wished to attain was reached. Here to our disappointment we discovered that what from above appeared a small break was in reality an overhanging face 15 feet high.'[5]

With modern climbing equipment it is not difficult to overcome such a break, but they could not see how they could climb this obstacle. They looked again towards the ridge 200 feet above them as the only route to the top. Fyfe thought they might try once more to gain it, this time by an adjacent rock face that was so steep there was little likelihood of it being loose. Once committed to the climb, it took them an hour before they got back onto the ridge which they found to be 'just climbable'. It was now 10.30 am, and they had not stopped since leaving the Hermitage at 3 am. Sitting high up on their rocky ridge and eating some of their remaining provisions, they could scan the valley below. Their fitness was not in question — they were going strongly — and the weather remained fine. The chances of success were good if their mountaineering skills and their nerves were equal to the task.

On the next section of climbing these were certainly tested to the full. Moving quickly up the rock ridge, they soon arrived at a place where an ice couloir straddled their path and fell steeply away to the Eugenie Glacier. It consisted of ice covered with two feet of soft snow, with the likelihood of the whole soft upper mass shooting off to the glacier if it was trodden or disturbed. Fyfe asked Graham to belay him with great care while he first cleared the soft snow and then began cutting steps into the ice. He calmly cut a line of steps across the very pronounced angle and later wrote of the incident: 'The couloir was so steep that the

66

back of the steps had to be cut fully 18 inches into the clear ice. When almost across, the whole of the snow lying below us went avalanching off with a hiss, completely baring the slope — the snow above luckily held.'[6] As they overcame each obstacle their determination to reach the summit strengthened.

Now they were rewarded with an easy climb across a basin to a saddle with glorious views of both the eastern and western sides of the alps. Of this Fyfe enthusiastically remarked, 'The sight as we topped the crest, was one long to be remembered. To our right toward the mighty Aorangi, with its hanging glaciers gloriously tinted by the noonday sun. Right at our feet lay the Copland, a tributary of the Karangarua River, at the mouth of which could be distinguished the white line of breakers rolling shoreward.'[7]

This was the first ascent on the Main Divide between Barron Saddle and Harper Saddle at the head of the Hooker Glacier, and it placed these two climbers in the most advantageous position up until that time to judge possible routes that might lead to Mt Cook and to the West Coast. It was also the first attempt to climb any of these peaks on the Main Divide. After enjoying the view, they descended a few hundred feet towards the west and moved along the ridge until they had gained a point closer to the summit. Here they showed their preference for rock climbing over step cutting, having done a good deal of the latter while ascending towards the Main Divide, and with the rock strata lying at an advantageous angle for holds, they made faster progress than had been possible for some hours. After trudging through snow, such moments of moving on rock can be blissful as the feet feel lighter.

However, in keeping with The Footstool's subsequent reputation for rotten rock, about 500 feet from the summit their route became extremely unstable again, rocks falling in masses at their touch. One piece went racing down and struck George Graham's head, unprotected by a helmet such as present-day climbers use. Fyfe wrote: 'It inflicted a nasty wound ... the blow was a severe one and I was doubtful if he could proceed any further.' Such blows are capable of unsettling climbers psychologically as well as physically. However, Graham was a tough and determined man, and as Fyfe wrote, 'pulling himself together he said he was quite capable of doing the remainder, so upward we toiled'.[8]

To have gone so far in one day and then given up so close to the summit would have been very disappointing. They looked carefully at the last steep section of ridge and then moved on to it. Of this decision Fyfe said that 'with the rock so terrible, and had we not been so near the top we would indubitably have turned back'. Climbers have to assess the risks of long exposure to rotten rock; in this instance they decided to climb on, but the comment gives some insight into Tom Fyfe's climbing philosophy. Summits were not the total objective; the enjoyment of climbing as safely as possible was of paramount importance and he was quite prepared to turn back if the dangers were too great. So, having assessed the risks, they moved up towards the summit of the peak.

Fyfe described the summit and the view which they were the first to see:

> The final pinch was very steep; but at last, after eleven hours' steady climbing, we stood on the top. So sharp was the ridge that had there been wind it would have been impossible for us to stand upright. The panoramic view that we now beheld was one of marvellous beauty and grandeur. By far the most conspicuous peak was Mt Sefton, which, on the side fronting us, was a sheer rock face, of, I should say over 2,000 feet. Bank's Range and Bank's Peak lay right at our feet, the lower slopes all being covered with bush, and forming quite a pleasing contrast to the bleak rocky valleys of Canterbury. Clustering around, and sunk into comparative insignificance by the majestic Aorangi, were Mt Stokes, Mt Dampier, St David's Dome, and the beautiful Silberhorn of Tasman just peeping out from behind. Over the Mt Cook Range could be seen the whole of the Malte Brun, and part of the Liebig Range, the Hochstetter Dome, and peaks innumerable at the head of the Murchison Glacier. Looking east were Lakes

The Mueller Glacier, photographed by Fyfe from The Footstool on 31 January 1894. This was the first photograph taken from a high summit in the Mt Cook area. The steepness of the summit cone of The Footstool is seen bottom right.

Photo: T.C. Fyfe, in Kinsey Collection, Canterbury Museum

Tekapo and Pukaki, with the Grampians away in the far background. Southward the view was unbounded, peak after peak appearing until they faded away with the softening mists of distance upon them.[9]

They could be proud of their achievement as the ascent of The Footstool from the valley floor entails a vertical distance of 7,000 feet. They had climbed it in eleven hours, a good climbing pace.

While on the summit they recorded their visit. Graham took bearings and Fyfe obtained some photographs with his camera, the first documented occasion when photographs had been taken from the summit of a high mountain in New Zealand. The technology of photography had changed from the wet-plate method used by the pioneering E.P. Sealy in the late 1860s which required a dark tent and a variety of chemicals to be at hand, and then the developing and fixing of the plate within minutes of the picture being taken. Twenty years later Arthur Harper was using dry-plate methods, which although more convenient still added considerably to a climber's load: fifteen

69

half-size plates, plus the camera, weighed 15 1/4 lbs (7.03 kg). The hand-held but still bulky camera Tom Fyfe used on top of The Footstool was a further advance, taking up to 100 quarter-plate pictures on one strip of film. George Mannering was another keen alpine photographer, as was Malcolm Ross. One of the first trips that George Graham did as a Hermitage guide was with George Moodie, a photographer employed by the well-known Burton Brothers of Dunedin. Moodie was at the Hermitage for seven weeks and it was Graham's job to transport eleven dozen large glass plates, dark tent, cameras, other gear and provisions to the Tasman, Hooker and Mueller Glaciers.

After Fyfe and Graham had recorded their achievement, they had a well-earned rest and then began the descent at 2.45 pm. Great care was needed immediately because the summit rock step of the peak is vertical. Fyfe anchored and Graham clambered down the rope, protected from the worst effects of a fall by being on a tight rope from above. Graham then anchored and Fyfe climbed down to him, and then anchored again while Graham climbed down. The climbing order indicates the confidence Tom Fyfe had in his own ability. After getting off this rocky ridge they tested the snow slopes for texture to see if they could glissade them, and finding the snow to their liking quickly lost height towards the saddle they had reached on the ascent.

It began to get colder, and on reaching the couloir they had crossed by cutting steps on the ascent, they found that the water which had collected in the steps during the sunny part of the day had turned to ice, so they soon took to the rocks again. They went down the rock ridge for about an hour and then decided to descend the glacier which would offer a direct approach to easier snow slopes. They managed to climb onto the snow, and with one anchoring and the other moving downwards they kept on the glacier until forced off it by the schrunds. With the rotten rock of the ridge now well behind, they began glissading down the snow slopes towards the Hermitage.

Adamson had watched them ascend the mountain and had seen them on top as dots against the blue sky. He welcomed them back at 9 pm, just as darkness fell across the valley floor. They

In this photograph that he took looking northward from The Footstool towards Mt Cook, Fyfe captured good views of the route to its summit that he later pioneered.
Photo: T.C. Fyfe, Aorangi from The Footstool, February 1894, in Kinsey Collection, Canterbury Museum

had been away for eighteen hours. Such ascents still test the fitness and stamina of climbers today. Indeed most ascents of The Footstool are now made not from the valley floor but from an altitude of 4,500 feet, where climbers can enjoy the comfort of the Sefton bivvy, a small hut on the mountain. For Fyfe and Graham this climb established a partnership, and the 1893-94 season became remarkable for the first ascents they achieved .

Fyfe sent the photographs taken from the summit of The Foot-stool to G.J. Roberts of the Westland Land Office. He knew that Roberts wanted information on the slopes above the area explored by C. E. Douglas in the Copland valley in order to make a map of the area. The completed map was then sent across to the Hermitage where it had been requested by Frank Huddleston, who wanted to see parties go over the Main Divide to the West Coast. With the map went the proviso that it was to be hung up at the Hermitage for the benefit of the public.

From The Footstool Fyfe and Graham had been able to look down, as no one had previously, onto possible passes in the south which might lead to the West Coast. Fyfe was now in a good position to explore the head of the Mueller Glacier as a feasible route to the West Coast for visitors to the Hermitage.

1. C. E. Collins, "Forgotten Pioneer of Mt Cook," *NZAJ* Vol. 30, (1977): 122-26.
2. T. C. Fyfe, "The Ascent of The Footstool," *NZAJ* Vol.1, No. 5, (May 1894): 268-275.
3. *Ibid.*
4. *Ibid.*
5. *Ibid.*
6. *Ibid.*
7. *Ibid.*
8. *Ibid.*
9. *Ibid.*

6

PEAKS, PASSES AND PIONEERING

The Main Divide of the Southern Alps is so rugged that along the hundreds of miles of its continuous length there are not more than about twelve well-defined passes. A glacier may rise to a high rounded saddle, yet be bunkered by deep crevasses. At other points there may be a mere notch in the rock face sufficient to let only one person through at a time. On the western side of the divide are deep swiftly flowing rivers that pass through rock, dense bush and huge boulders and make passage so difficult as to frustrate even the most ardent and skilled mountaineers. In addition a crossing requires experience and good judgement about the weather. Within an hour a clear blue sky can change to dull grey, heralding rain and snow.

Many of the high alpine passes carry the names of their earliest European visitors: Browning Pass at the head of the Wilberforce River, Whitcombe Pass near the headwaters of the Rakaia River, Graham Saddle at the division of the Rudolf and the Franz Josef Glaciers, Sealy Pass at the separation of the Godley Glacier from the remote areas of the Perth, and the well-known Copland Pass — a tiny depression in the rock and ice wall that stands between the Hooker valley at Mt Cook and the Copland valley on the West Coast. A little further south Fyfe Pass and Brodrick Pass provide access to South Westland.

In the 1890s, however, if visitors to the Hermitage had wished to continue over to the West Coast they would have had to travel long distances, over either the Sealy Pass rising out of the Godley Glacier to the north or Brodrick Pass to the south. The owners of the Hermitage, and especially Frank Huddleston, wanted people to be able to cross the Main Divide near the Hermitage, so that they would be more likely to include the hotel and its attractions in their travel plans. A pass that linked the Mt Cook area with South Westland needed to be easily negotiated, and safe from avalanche danger and rockfall.

Huddleston had been told by G.J. Roberts of the Westland Land Office that a possible route existed in the Copland valley: 'In 1880 the trig surveyor made a topographical study of the Divide, etc, from station J.M. and especially noted a double depression at the head of the Copland Valley'.[1] Later Charles Douglas also saw the small depressions referred to by the surveyor but thought the height and the rough nature of the climb on the Mt Cook side made it unsuitable.

As late as December 1893 no one had crossed over to the West Coast from the Hermitage. Visitors to the region who wished to go to the West Coast were still having to retrace their steps to Christchurch and go by coach over Arthur's Pass. At the beginning of the next year Fyfe proposed to George Graham that they explore a route to link the two sides of the alps. With an eye to the commercial interest of the Hermitage, they decided to take a camera even though it would add considerably to their swags. Having already viewed the Copland route from a high vantage point, Fyfe decided to try to cross further to the south where on previous expeditions he had noted the possibility of a pass near the head of the Mueller Glacier.

By the beginning of February 1894 all was in readiness — blankets, climbing rope, camera, extra clothing and food all packed into swags. Also included was a shortened version of the skis that Marmaduke Dixon had devised for making it easier to travel on soft snow in attempts on Mt Cook.[2] Fyfe and Graham planned to be away for nine days, beginning with a climb up the Mueller Glacier in the direction of Barron Saddle, wondering, no doubt, what lay beyond the 5,000 foot wall of rock and ice that separates east from west.

The Mueller is a vast ice flow which begins at the southern end of what is now the Mt Cook National Park and approaches the Hermitage in a giant crescent shape, depositing its terminal moraine near the site of the first hotel. The glacier collects snow and ice from the jagged peaks that rise on the Main Divide where Eagle Peak and Maunga Ma form part of a crenellated barrier extending from Mt Sefton to Mt Burns. To the west beyond this wall of snow and rock lie the Douglas, Fyfe and McKerrow

Glaciers that even today remain isolated and a challenge to mountaineers.

Facing the long climb up the Mueller Glacier, Fyfe and Graham got onto their skis — the first recorded instance of their being used on the Mueller Glacier. It was a good decision because by day's end they found themselves at the head of the glacier, having covered the distance with some ease. When they had established their camp on the névé near Barron Saddle they were in a good position to attempt some climbing and try to find a pass. The *Timaru Herald* records that they tried to climb Mt Sealy but found the approach they were on not to their liking. Some years later Tom Fyfe's comment to the newspaper that it was a 'terror to climb' was quoted back at him in a derisory way by the English climber, Edward Fitzgerald in his book.[3] (Having made a special trip to New Zealand, Fitzgerald was piqued at not being the first to climb Mt Cook.)

Frustrated by the poor quality of the rock on Mt Sealy, Fyfe and Graham now set about reconnoitring a way down to the West Coast. After some time they discovered what appeared to be a possible pass, which Fyfe described as 'a narrow gap bounded by Mt Montgommery [sic] on the south and a sheer rock face of I should say 1000 feet on the north'.[4] It was duly named Fyfe Pass. On its eastern side a snow slope extends well up to it, but its western aspect offers a wide and often bare rock face. The lack of easily identifiable features on this face was to cause them much trouble later.

The terrain now spread out below them looked difficult and they

Here on the Mueller Glacier en route to the West Coast in February 1894, Fyfe has photographed Graham having difficulties using shortened skis. They were simply boards to which leather bindings were lashed.
Photos: T.C. Fyfe, Kinsey Album, Canterbury Museum.

75

Fyfe and Graham's campsite at the head of the Mueller Glacier in February 1894, looking towards Fyfe Pass, centre, and Mt Burns, right. The tent poles were ice axes turned on their heads with an extension added for height. This tent and its pegs were later abandoned in the Landsborough valley.

Photo: T.C. Fyfe, Kinsey Collection, Canterbury Museum

decided that no place looked better than any other, and so made use of a very narrow couloir which appeared to run down towards the glacier below. Climbing very carefully down to what Fyfe referred to as the Two Thumb Glacier but which is now known as the Spence Glacier, they finally reached the valley. The tension of the descent now lifted and they felt elated and relieved after a successful and incident-free first crossing. They made a tent camp about two miles below the terminal moraine of the McKerrow Glacier. Next morning, with the weather still marvellously fine, the prospect of a complete crossing beckoned and they tried to descend the Landsborough River, only to find it ran into a very deep gorge with a rough bottom. The terrain was extremely rugged and Fyfe recalled that the five miles down and back made for a hard day's work.

Having their immediate plans thwarted, they decided the next day to climb up the McKerrow Glacier where to their delight they found good walking on clean ice. They climbed well up the glacier and then turned towards the west and gained the saddle which is now known as Douglas Pass. This leads into the head of the Douglas River, a tributary of the Karangarua River which

The terrain over which Fyfe and Graham climbed from the Mueller Glacier to the McKerrow Glacier in February 1894. Fyfe Pass lies between Mt Montgomery, left, and Scissors, centre.
Photo: Gavin Wills

enters the sea some distance south of Gillespies Beach. The pass presented no difficulties, and they descended towards the river through snow grass and stunted scrub. It was the type of country which Fyfe thought would be traversable by a tourist track, especially since Charles Douglas had earlier made his way from the West Coast side to the foot of the saddle they had just descended.

In linking Douglas's route with their own they had thus succeeded in discovering a new route from the Hermitage to the West Coast and in making the first crossing of the Main Divide in the Mt Cook area. Fyfe estimated the distance from the camp two miles below the McKerrow Glacier to the foot of the Douglas Pass to be about six miles. With this in mind he thought that a horse track could be cut up the east side of the Mueller Glacier and that a short day's walk would then take visitors to the Douglas Valley. The possibility of this as a regular route appears not to have been considered further, but given the length of the journey it is not surprising.

They were now getting desperately short of food, and inquisitive kea became a tempting target. Fyfe wrote later: 'We had been in the Landsborough three days and of tucker there was never a vestige in the camp. On the evening of our last night we managed to secure a kea. As it was very cold we had turned into our sleeping bags early, and were quietly enjoying a last pipe in lieu of supper when this unfortunate bird luckily came poking around the tent. Not even waiting to clothe himself and with a bloodthirsty look of determination Graham crept out into the frosty night and in a few minutes returned exultantly dangling his spoil by the neck. After what appeared to be hours of boiling although eventually when back in a land of plenty we unashamedly confessed that that it could only have been minutes, we divided the game and there was a sound as of gnawing and smacking of lips far into the stilly night. This case of "overfeeding" occurred about midnight and bar another kea was our last hope of food on that side of the divide.'[5]

They had been living under canvas and making bush camps for over a week, and in the kind of good weather which, when it

It was over this range of mountains that Fyfe and Graham climbed in their journey to the West Coast in February 1894. In this 1967 photo-graph J. Smith and O. Bunce are on Douglas Pass, first crossed by Fyfe and Graham.

Photo: R. Barrack

occurs on the West Coast, is sheer delight — glorious scenery, low rivers, warm tussock and the sweet smell of the forest. Because they were so short of food, however, their thoughts now turned towards the journey back to the Hermitage. They planned it would be by the way they had arrived in the Landsborough, if the same crossing point could be found again in the mountain wall. As it turned out this proved difficult, mainly because the weather now turned against them.

Tom Fyfe described the scene and their preparations thus: 'With the dawn came rain — a good sample of West Coast rain. Rain or no rain we had to make the Hermitage and after waiting until 7 am we struck camp. Our swags were light. We sacrificed a tent, billy, blankets and a tomahawk. This left Graham with only his sleeping bag and blankets, whilst I had as ballast a perfect beauty of a camera which weighed 14lbs without plates. It was not so much the weight of the machine as the beastly trick it had of finding out the soft places, and sometimes in fancy even yet I feel its sharp corners digging into my back. I modestly suggested to Graham that perhaps we should have quite enough to carry if he left his swag and took turn about with the camera; but they were his blankets and he replied that "when he got to the Hermitage his swag would". It did not.'[6]

To Fyfe's disappointment, the camera remained in his own

79

swag, and in pouring rain they turned their faces towards the east and home. Keeping close to the lateral moraine of the glacier they made their way down the valley. With Fyfe Pass but a narrow gap between Mt Montgomery and the adjoining rock face, and now covered in dense cloud, it was difficult to locate it. This experience led Fyfe to write later of the pass, 'It oftimes proved most difficult to find', which points to their being in the region more than once in later years. They were now looking for the narrow snow and rock couloir which leads to the pass, just one of the many couloirs in the area. They started by climbing a rock face which they believed led to the couloir and continued up it for some time, hoping it would lead them towards the pass.

At one point as they were trying to climb a particularly steep section George Graham thought the rock also contained his future wealth. Fyfe said, 'I was startled by Graham who was a few feet away yelling Gold! Gold! Joining him I could see just beyond our reach something of a dull yellowish colour — was it gold? To mount on Graham's shoulders and reach his find was but the work of a moment and then came the disillusion. It was mundic — large cubes firmly embedded and projecting out of the rock. Our find was at least some value as these cubes presented fairly good footholds and with their aid we scrambled out of the couloir.'[7] (Mundic is the name given by Cornish miners to iron pyrites.)

They now found the conditions very demanding. The constant rain meant it was difficult to get a firm hold on the rock face, and the ice in the couloirs hardened and required a lot of step cutting. At one point, not knowing if they were on the correct route, they traversed the rock in an attempt to find the couloir that led to the pass up which an ascent could be made. It could not be found. Now high up on the range and with no prospect of food back in the valley, retreat was unthinkable, so with thoughts only of the fare available at the Hermitage their course continued upwards. As they climbed higher the rock lay back to an angle of 45°, and they gradually inched their way forward. Fyfe wrote: 'Our hands and knees became raw leaving a trail of blood. Our swags though light, swayed and chafed us beyond all endurance and added to this was the discouraging fact that we knew not where if at all we should strike the divide.'[8]

However, as on many occasions, their perseverance and fitness pulled them through. Late in the day, after hours of struggle, they finally stood on the Main Divide once more, but they had no idea at which point they had reached it. However, although it was still raining, far beneath them in the gloom they could see the Mueller Glacier — familiar territory and the way back to the Hermitage. Still uncertain as to exactly where they were, they guessed that they had reached a point about half a mile south of Fyfe Pass.

Though tired and very hungry, Fyfe retained the teasing sense of humour he was to become known for in difficult situations in the years ahead. They had agreed on the route they would take off the divide and were about to begin the descent, when George Graham, instead of shouldering his swag, began unravelling it. Of this Fyfe wrote: 'On my inquiry he informed me in a most graphic manner that it was his intention to leave it there. I at first remonstrated with him, pointing out that now he had carried it so far he might as well bring it the rest of the way. But no — hanging the blankets over a ledge he proceeded to fix them by placing rocks on the corners.'[9] Fyfe reminded Graham that he had promised to take the blankets back to the Hermitage. But the blankets stayed there, and Fyfe recalled the incident: 'This was the last straw and our sublime mountains were desecrated by language positively unprintable. He even went so far as to renounce mountaineering in general and the company of mountaineers who in Graham's estimation required a stronger word than fools to fully describe them.'[10]

With little further talk passing between them, they commenced climbing carefully down the steep rock face and finally reached the glacier late in the afternoon without incident. The snow and glacial ice of the Mueller stretched out before them, but on stopping to fill their pipes they turned and looking back to where they had been, saw to their surprise that Graham's blankets were clearly visible high above them blowing in the wind from the summit of Mt Montgomery, the

PIERCING THE CLOUDS

first ascent of which they now realised they had just made.

When Fyfe wrote his account of this expedition to J.J. Kinsey in November 1897, he and other New Zealand climbers had cause to recall Edward Fitzgerald's comments in his account of his climbing in New Zealand, published in 1897. Fyfe and Graham were well known for their ability to travel long distances quickly, and in rebuttal of Fitzgerald's comments that New Zealand climbers carried too much food, Fyfe completed his account of the journey by saying: 'We sighted the welcome lights of the Hermitage at 9 pm and were soon regaling ourselves with a basin of gruel. Altogether on this "little expedition" we were 32 hours with only a kea to keep us alive and out of this 32 hours

Mountains and bush on the West Coast damage clothing and footwear. A.P. Harper uses a stone to repair his boot, 1890s.
Source: J.J. Kinsey Collection, Canterbury Museum

82

were on the move 20. I think I can safely state that there was no "overfeeding" on this excursion and strange to relate we were "going strong" when we finished. Indeed one of the party sat up until some time after midnight playing whist. N.B. This is what is commonly called "skite" but I cannot after all the hungry days I have spent get over that charge of overfeeding. Likewise I am willing to back at least three New Zealanders for all I am worth to go further and longer without food than the author of the above charge.'[11]

Fyfe and Graham had reason to be well satisfied with the results of the journey. They had crossed the Main Divide from the Hermitage for the first time, descending well into Westland, and in the process had explored a lot of territory, which Charles Douglas and Arthur Harper investigated further the following year. However, the Department of Lands and Survey's specification of a 'mule pass free from ice between the Hermitage and the West Coast' had not been met and the quest continued. W. G. McClymont wrote of these attempts in his book, *The Exploration of New Zealand,* noting that 'Douglas was assisted by A.P. Harper who had been one of the enterprising amateurs climbing in the Mt Cook region' and that 'they decided to explore the Karangarua' in 1894-1895, 'and go over the hills to the Landsborough from where Brodrick Pass led to the Huxley River and Lake Ohau. They started but Douglas, broken by his past exertions, returned, and Harper went to the Landsborough and down to the Haast with a Maori porter. They returned by much the same route and reported that a route to Lake Ohau was feasible but too long for tourists. The Department decided that Harper should re-explore the Copland for a pass not necessarily free from ice.'[12] Fyfe and Graham had considered the possibility of a pass between the Hooker and the Copland valleys in their ascent of The Footstool, and they had subsequently looked further to the south, for, as Douglas had told the Department, referring to a pass at the head of the Copland River, 'they could have a road only if it went over a sloping icefield swept by avalanches or under the glacier by tunnel'.

Buoyed by their success, Fyfe and Graham now turned their attention towards a further attempt on Mt De la Beche, the eleventh by New Zealand mountaineers. Fyfe was among those who had been defeated earlier, and clearly the peak still held much attraction for him. Some weeks previously Malcolm Ross together with two other aspirant climbers, Gibbs and Wilson, had reached quite a high level on the mountain only to find they could not negotiate the crevasses and schrunds and were forced to abandon the climb. By way of consolation they attempted an ascent of the Rudolf Glacier to the saddle which divides it from the Franz Josef Glacier, but when they were within eighty or ninety yards of their objective two of the party fell into crevasses and that ascent was also aborted.

On the morning of 15 February 1894, less than a week after their previous trip, Fyfe and Graham departed for the Tasman Glacier. They were in fine physical condition from their long journey over to the West Coast, and they reached the De la Beche bivouac in time to set up camp before nightfall. A heavy fog hung around the peak and the possibility of bad weather meant they had some spare time at their disposal. Deciding to climb on the 16th, they walked across the Tasman Glacier to gather a supply of firewood from the scrub on the Malte Brun Range which at that time served as fuel to supplement the firewood carried up to the bivouac.

In the hope of a first ascent of Mt De la Beche, they left the bivouac site at 4.25 am and climbed up the Rudolf Glacier, following the same route as other parties on previous attempts. Although the glacier acts as a receptacle for all the rock and ice that falls from precipitous slopes of the Main Divide to the south-west, it presented good walking until the icefall in the middle was reached. Here they crossed to the true left and began climbing the rock, at that point a series of small buttresses. After climbing up these without difficulty for two hours, they found they could again move out onto the glacier. The ice now required steps to be cut up each pitch, and although the angle of this slope is not steep, the number of crevasses, in late summer, meant that they had to choose a route carefully. With the prospect of success and of seeing what mountains lay on the other side of the saddle they were now approaching, they made the pace a fast one.

At 8.30 am they finally stood on the crest of the ridge between the Rudolf and Franz Josef Glaciers, the first persons to do so. George Graham, after whom this high alpine saddle was later named, wrote of the view: 'From this point the coastline was visible under a heavy rolling fog, and directly below us was a great basin crossed in all directions with crevasses, especially at the outlet, where it seemed to drop sharply, this being probably the head of the icefall.' They had climbed quickly and were keen to keep going lest the fog envelop their objective, but found that there were some difficult sections on it, as Graham explained: 'After a 15 minute spell we turned to the peak, keeping straight up a snow-slope to the edge of an immense schrund, the upper lip of which was fully 50 feet above where we stood. At one end the ice had fallen in and partly filled the gap, and over this we managed to scramble, cutting a few steps up the face until we reached the rock above. At first it was very rotten but improved higher up, and although it was extremely steep and in some places very awkward, taking it all through we made good speed. Halfway up from the snow slope we struck into a couloir, which seemed to be the best route, and up this we worked our passage, till, after a final scramble over loose rock, we stood on the highest pinnacle, and looked down onto the Tasman — time, 10.20 am.'[13]

The completion of this climb in just under six hours without crampons shows how quickly they moved; many parties since have taken somewhere near this to get no further than Graham Saddle. Their performance points to the increasing confidence and competence that this pioneering pair were acquiring in moving on mixed snow and rock and in overcoming relatively steep rock on high peaks with their adjacent and sometimes problematic schrunds. Graham wrote: 'From start to finish we went "all we knew", and with the exception of a 15 minute spell on the Rudolf Saddle we scarcely stopped for breath from the start.'

Atop another virgin peak, they had the honour of building a cairn, and in a jam jar they recorded their ascent. Having decided to carry as little equipment as possible, they had forsaken the camera in the quest for speed on the climb.

85

However, from the summit there was the majestic view, the peak being surrounded on all sides by large glaciers and other mountains. To the north Elie de Beaumont rose spectacularly for 4,000 feet from the Spencer Glacier, its steep icy faces and rock ridges making an impregnable fortress. To the east lay a battalion of mountains on the Malte Brun Range — all unclimbed at that time. Adjacent and just to the north were the tantalising slopes of the Minarets.

Tom Fyfe, keen to climb the Minarets as well as Mt De la Beche, suggested this to Graham, and to test the firmness of the steep snow slope on the Tasman side of this peak which they would need to descend to get nearer, they threw rocks down it. When this started a minor avalanche — probably because this faces east and catches the morning sun — they decided to be satisfied with their ascent of De la Beche. Reluctantly they took a last look at the magnificent view, and then turned and started retracing their steps with great care. On reaching the head of the Rudolf Glacier and its attendant icefall at the point where the rock climbing could be avoided, they altered course. It was at this steep piece of rock in an icy gully that R.B. Low, an English climber, later fell in 1906. Having descended the glacier above, Low then began an epic three-day crawl along the miles of glacier and moraine, dragging a broken ankle until he reached shelter at the De la Beche bivouac rock. No such mishap befell Fyfe and Graham, but the latter remarked that the 'snow throughout was as hard as glass, and glissading was entirely out of the question'.[14] Quite against their wishes, they had to descend the rock to the bottom of the icefall, arriving back at their camp at 4 pm.

Their safe return at the end of a brilliant February day drew down the curtain on an important first ascent in the heart of unclimbed peaks in the Tasman Glacier area. Following their fast climb and the walk out to the Hermitage, Tom Fyfe decided on a few days' rest. George Graham, however, returned up the Tasman Glacier, there guiding Dr Cox of Christchurch and his party on a climb of Hochstetter Dome. During this trip of four to five days the party made the ascent of that peak in perfect climbing conditions and without having to cut a step with the ice axe. In the era when crampons were not being used at the Hermitage, and hard snow or ice necessitated staircases of cutting, such an ascent was most unusual.

1. G.J. Roberts, *Westland: New Zealand Tours and Excursions* (Wellington: 1898), pp.42-3.
2. Record of qualifications of members on election to New Zealand Alpine Club 1891. Hocken Library.
3. *Timaru Herald,* 30 March 1894.
4. T.C. Fyfe. Unpublished account of the first crossing of the Fyfe and Douglas Passes. Alexander Turnbull Library.
5. *Ibid.*
6. *Ibid.*
7. *Ibid.*
8. *Ibid.*
9. *Ibid.*
10. *Ibid.*
11. *Ibid.*
12. W.G. McClymont, *The Exploration of New Zealand* 2nd ed., (London: Oxford University Press, 1959), p.106.
13. M. Ross, "The Ascent of Mt De La Beche," *NZAJ* Vol. 1, No. 5, (May 1894): 275-281.
14. *Ibid.*

7

SOLO ON MALTE BRUN

In mountaineering history there are few instances of solo ascents of high virgin peaks, but two are well known. In January 1897 at the age of forty-one Mattias Zurbriggen climbed alone up the final 1700 feet of Mt Aconcagua (23,400 ft), South America's highest peak. And in July 1953, just weeks after the first ascent of Mt Everest, Hermann Buhl made a solo ascent of last 4,000 feet of the Himalayan giant, Nanga Parbat (26,620 ft). Solo climbing is often discouraged, and on high virgin summits there is the added danger of the unknown. Safety is the most obvious issue, but perhaps the most interesting question is the motivation of the climber taking risks. How do climbers gain such confidence in their abilities? And what prompts them to make the attempt? Is it the sheer challenge to technical skill, or is it a matter of personal ambition, the prospect of fame and reputation?

When Tom Fyfe set off alone to climb the 10,000 foot Malte Brun, no party or individual had ascended a New Zealand peak of that height. Did he have sufficient experience and judgement to minimise the risks? He lacked the expert instruction available to Europeans, but in three years he had proved to be an apt learner from those around him and from his own experience. His climbing skills were highly regarded and he was known as an innovator and a good judge of routes. What then of his motivation: was it the challenge of the peak itself or was it the possibility of fame? The story of his full climbing career suggests the former.

All that survives of his own explanation is this: 'To most mountaineers an apology for climbing alone will appear necessary, but I have none to offer, and fail to see that solitary climbing is, on rock peaks, so foolhardy as authorities would have us believe. Foolhardy or not, it has a fascination that is entirely wanting when climbing in company.'[1] That view was contrary to the normal practice of his day. Fyfe accepted the climbing conventions of the 1890s, but he was quick to modify those that he believed needed to be modified. He was always looking for new ways of climbing without compromising safety. He felt prepared for tackling a significant peak alone because of the solo climbing he had done on reconnaissance trips, and he did limit his approval to climbing on rock as distinct from snow and ice.

New Zealand's highest mountains are known mainly for what they offer the snow and ice climber, and only a few areas, notably the Darren Mountains, contain really sound rock. However, some difficult rock climbing is available on Malte Brun and the other peaks of that range. East of the Main Divide, it receives less snow from the prevailing westerly quarter than other peaks in the region, which means that its western flanks present high rock faces and steep ridges often relatively free of snow. Viewed from the Mackenzie basin, Malte Brun stands out from its neighbours — Mts Hamilton, Aiguilles Rouges and Chudleigh. At daylight on a fine morning it may be seen to marvellous effect. As the sun strikes its high rock faces and summit, the mountain emits a red glow, and gradually the whole peak is spectacularly revealed in its dawn colours. It has a distinctive shape viewed from either east or west, its fluted colonnades of rock merging together to form a narrow summit apex. Its uniformly steep battlements are guarded at their bases by five attendant glaciers, the Bonney and Darwin to the north-west, the Beetham to the south, the Cascade Glacier to the south-east and the Baker directly east. Late in the climbing season access onto the mountain can be a problem, but once it is gained the absence of snow on the rock is of course an advantage. Until Fyfe's attempt, however, all this was unknown.

The De la Beche bivouac was the base for his climb. By starting from the Tasman Glacier, that is, the western side, Fyfe was able to unravel some of the glacial geography of the area. On 7 March 1894 he assessed the weather as being settled, the rock free of snow and the hours of daylight long enough. He set off at 4.45 am — not especially early — and climbed quickly up the lateral moraine which at that time did not drop away several hundred feet into the glacier as it does today. After pausing for a moment near the icefall, Fyfe found that he was able to move quickly up and across the ice of the Tasman Glacier. Within half an hour, and moving at a brisk pace, he had positioned himself by dawn to be in the vicinity of a spur which was his chosen reference point to begin the ascent.

From here he planned to climb the buttress in front of the main peak, which divides at its base into the spur he had arrived at. If he could reach this, he believed, he would be in a good position to climb the North Ridge which commences from the Bonney Glacier just above a small icefall. This spur, however, runs to a narrow point with steep sides dropping to the Darwin Glacier, and as he climbed up it he found he was separated from the North Ridge by a series of large crevasses in the Bonney Glacier. But all was not lost, for on reaching a prominent point at 7.40 am he was greeted for the first time with a glimpse of the true extent and majesty of the Darwin Glacier which feeds into the Tasman Glacier in a giant crescent shape. From this viewpoint Fyfe was also able to assess for future climbing the most convenient route that might be taken in any attempt on Mt Darwin. He had gained the spur in just over an hour's climbing on good firm rock. Now he was forced onto some hard snow that required cutting with the pick end of the ice axe before he could negotiate the final parts of the spur. He applied himself to this task only to see his chances of reaching the North Ridge disappear as he was confronted by a vast web of deep crevasses. They spelled danger and the loss of precious time if crossed alone.

One element of successful mountaineering is the willingness to discard an intended climbing route in favour of a different approach when necessary. Tom Fyfe had that flexibility, underpinned by a fierce determination not to be beaten by the mountain. He later recalled that he was reluctantly coming to the conclusion that he had failed, when he conceived the idea of scaling the peak up the vertical-looking face in front of him — the face that rises steeply out of the Bonney Glacier for nearly 2000 feet. Like the whole mountain, it was then unattempted and unknown.

Fyfe thought that what he could see of the face resembled the upper section of the rock climb he and George Graham had done on Mt De la Beche, and this was sufficient to persuade him to proceed. It was that combination of skill and judgment that later

Malte Brun which
Fyfe climbed in a
solo and first
ascent, following
the ridge in the
centre and contin-
uing up the West
Face to the summit.
Photo: Maurice Conway.

drew from Jack Clark the comment that Fyfe was a 'climber to his
fingertips',[2] and later still Peter Graham's evaluation: 'I have
always considered him the finest of our early mountaineers.'[3]
Physical strength and fitness were important factors also. Fyfe
trained for mountaineering as athletes train for their events. He
lifted weights to improve his arm strength and he worked on his
balance as well, jumping from one suspended beam to another,
as a gymnast might.[4] Frequent guiding work and carrying heavy
loads also helped to keep him in top condition. However,
physical endurance, although important, is of limited use in
serious mountaineering if it is not accompanied by a steady
nerve and a head for heights. It was this combination that gave
Fyfe the confidence to tackle the steep climb in front of him.

Before reaching the base of the climb from his newly-won vantage point at 8,700 feet, however, he had first to climb down a snow slope for several hundred feet. On doing so he was shortly confronted by a deep bergschrund that seemed to be too wide to jump. Ingenuity and confidence were now needed if a leap across the huge void was to be accomplished. Taking a heavy stone in each hand for extra momentum, he sprang across the depths from a standing start, landing safely in the snow on the other side of the bergschrund. This placed him in a position to attempt to cross the next section of crevasses, after which the start of the rock climb could be reached.

In the 1890s the usual technique adopted for crossing crevassed glaciers was for the climber following the lead climber to keep the rope between them very taut, so that any fall into a crevasse might be held. Climbing alone in crevassed areas of course presents greater risks of a fall, perhaps a fatal one, into the black depths of the glacier. To deal with the problem of having no one to hold him if he broke through, Fyfe had developed a way of using his ice axe as a stake in the snow to hold his weight. He now used this to good effect, explaining later: 'In crossing the basin or plateau I had one or two crevasses to deal with, and made use of my axe as an anchor before going forward to test them, passing the rope around the ice axe and paying out an end as I moved forward.'[5] Having found the snow to be safe, he then retreated over the crevassed area to reclaim the axe before going on, obviously believing that the snow would hold his weight. Such are the risks that solo climbers take. Fyfe now moved across the glacier to where the face began.

Access from a glacier to a mountain is often impeded by bergschrunds, but snow couloirs sometimes connect the glacier and the rock as fingers are connected to a hand. Fyfe now looked carefully at possible couloirs, but all were subject to repeated rockfall and the most likely one seemed to be cut off by three small schrunds. He now moved to the north of these couloirs but was again unable to cross the bergschrund. Not to be defeated, he returned to the couloir cut by the three small schrunds and on reconsideration thought this provided the only opportunity of getting onto the rock face. He began climbing up the couloir as

View of Elie de Beaumont from the Bonney Glacier. During his ascent of Malte Brun, Fyfe was the first climber on this glacier.
Photo: Gotlieb Braun-Elwert, Alpine Recreation, (Canterbury) Ltd

far as the first schrund and found he was able to climb off onto the rock without having to cross the schrund. At this point there was a sharply angled overhanging rock that would require all his considerable agility to overcome. Beyond that the climb soared up in great slabs above him. Once committed to the climb there would be little opportunity to turn back.

Fyfe had prepared meticulously for the serious undertaking that now confronted him. The standard climbing footwear at the time was a pair of sturdy leather boots, nailed with metal studs for better grip and wear. The disadvantage of these was that they did not mould easily to the different contours of rock and it was difficult to get sufficient purchase on steep sections. To overcome this problem Fyfe had been experimenting with rubber-soled sports shoes which he found provided much better friction and grip on a rock surface. Now, taking off the boots he had worn so far, he changed into the shoes he had in his swag and began climbing up the steep rock face above him. He commented later, referring to his use of these shoes, that 'but for this, the peak would still be unclimbed', adding that 'they seem to get a safe hold almost anywhere, and on rock peaks the best climbers should go provided with one or more pairs'.[6] In 1912 Jim Dennistoun used similar footwear for the first ascent of Mitre Peak, but the practice went relatively unnoticed in New Zealand for a long time. It was not until the 1960s that rubber-soled boots called Kletters began to be used extensively for steep rock climbs.

As Fyfe progressed up the face the climbing became very demanding. He wrote: 'It was now real hand and foot climbing and a mistake could have been fatal. I kept away slightly to the left all the time, that being the lowest point of the top. The variety and difficulty of this climb was enough to satisfy any lover of rock work. A stratum of slatey rock running horizontally across the peak proved troublesome being very rotten and cutting my hands severely. At 12.40 pm, however, I stood on the lowest point of the peak, and Malte Brun was virtually conquered.'[7]

Crossing the small peaks which form the summit ridge, he quickly made his way to the top after cutting a few steps, and shortly reached the uppermost point of 10,421 feet. In doing so he had climbed the 5,000 feet required in just over six hours, the highest standard of rock climbing that had then been attempted in New Zealand. He had also become the first person in New Zealand to ascend to a summit over 10,000 feet high. And he had done so alone, without the protection on the face of a rope to avert a fall. It had been a unique and well planned climb, achieved with a mixture of skill and daring, and it had been undertaken on rock, the difficulties of which were unknown at that time.

Now on the summit, unprotected by the synthetic jackets and clothing with which today's climbers keep warm, he was struck by a bitterly cold southerly wind. There was time, however, to commemorate the achievement and to validate his summit claim. He built a cairn on one of the points and under it left a knife with his name and the date of the ascent, 7 March 1894, scratched on the bone handle. He then built a more solid cairn on a lower point and ate his first food since leaving the De la Beche bivouac. He later described the view from the summit: '...very grand, composed as it was of the most sublime objects, blended with or divided from each other in every variety that could gratify the eye and charm the imagination. At my feet lay our two greatest glaciers, the Tasman and the Murchison, with all their innumerable tributaries. Over the Mount Cook spur the Mueller could be surveyed for miles, whilst away north, peak after peak appeared until they were lost in the far distance'.[8]

However, as mountaineers are only too aware, when the summit is reached the climb is but half done. Fyfe stayed on the summit for forty-five minutes, and then, thinking he might improve the route taken on the ascent, he moved slightly to the south and down towards a couloir. The way was not easy and in various places he had to adopt the hazardous method, akin to modern abseiling, of passing the rope around a projecting rock and lowering himself over the rock faces. In a typical understatement he wrote that 'a slip here and I would have landed on the Darwin Glacier, 1,000 feet below, faster than would have been altogether pleasant'. He later became renowned as being one of the few people able to climb down the overhang on the North Ridge of Mount Cook.

He reached the couloir he was aiming for at the top of the snow and began climbing down it. Then began one of the best known and certainly the most dramatic descents of Malte Brun. 'After I had descended a short way, and when about 700 feet from where it ended, an ominous sound like the report of firearms warned me that I was in danger. Casting one look behind I saw several rocks starting to come right from the summit. My only chance was to beat those rocks down to the glacier, where the soft snow would bring them up. The couloir was steep, the snow hard, and by laying [sic] flat on my back, I simply went down as if falling through air. The small schrunds I do not remember crossing at all, for it was impossible to keep my eyes open. Coming quickly to my feet, I turned around just in time to see a whole shower of small stones burying themselves in the snow, and one or two large pieces rolling to my feet.'[9] He later wrote in the hut book at Ball Hut that he had 'played a lone hand with Malte and won'.

Now well off the peak, he made speed on the rest of the easy descent by glissades to the Tasman Glacier, reaching it at 3.50 pm, having taken only 2 hours 25 minutes from the summit. In all probability this time still stands as the fastest descent of the mountain. The whole climb remains remarkable, bearing comparison with climbs then being done in Europe, and outstanding for its boldness, the high standard of rock climbing it entailed and the speed of its execution. It was a 'free' climb, done solo, and may therefore be described as a 1980s style climb, but it was a century ahead of its time.

Jack Clark. At nineteen years of age he accompanied Tom Fyfe and George Graham on the first ascent of Mt Cook. Two months later, invited to join Edward Fitzgerald and Mattias Zurbriggen, he was on the first ascent of Mt Tasman, the first New Zealander on our second highest peak.
Source: Canterbury Museum.

Shortly after this ascent some visitors to the Hermitage wanted to do more than walk nearby tracks. A party was formed to climb Hochstetter Dome at the head of the Tasman Glacier: Mr and Mrs Maxwell of Hobart and Dr Franz Kronecker from Berlin, guided by Tom Fyfe, Jack Clark and Jack Adamson. Maxwell's description of the scene at the bivouac at the foot of Mt De la Beche is evocative of many a later climbing party's bivouac. 'Tea here was an interesting sight. Seated around the entrance were some of us, the rest under the rock. Candles stuck into the bottom of meat tins gave a flickering uncertain light, a flat stone served as a table, on which to spread our meal of bread, butter, tinned meat and jam with a heterogeneous collection of utensils, and all sorts of drinking vessels from a pannikin to an empty jam tin. The small fire a short distance away lit up the huge boulders around, and made the darkness beyond a deeper black, while on the mountains boomed the avalanches, echoing in the still evening.'[10] The guides and Kronecker were ensconced in the less than salubrious bivouac, packed close on straw mattresses, while Maxwell and his wife slept in a tent outside.

Large parties can be slow in departing for a climb; this one did no better, with a 5.15 am start. They had a slow journey up the Tasman Glacier under the hot summer sun with the glare reflected off the snow, and it was noon before they finally found their way onto Lendenfeld Saddle. There, in oppressive heat,

they took a break for lunch. Seeking some respite, Fyfe and the other guides drove their ice axes into the snow, suspended their coats over the heads of the axes and thus got some shade and rest. Jack Clark searched in his pack for the water-tin and was shame-faced to find that during the walk up the glacier it had got turned upside down and had silently emptied itself. So they had to resort to melting some snow.

They then began the ascent of the peak, but without Adamson who had injured himself the day before. Fyfe led in the usual guide's custom, cutting steps in the standard zigzag fashion up the steeper sections and across the bergschrunds. They encountered some difficult sections — bergschrunds and forty-foot-high ice walls — and Fyfe finally skirted around to the back of the peak and approached the final 150 feet from that direction. It was four o'clock in the afternoon before they began the descent from the summit, and it was a weary sunburnt party that reached the De la Beche bivouac at 9.30 pm, completing a sixteen-hour day. They had had some tedious work picking their way in the darkness among the ice hummocks of the glacier, and Jack Clark was sent on ahead to fetch a lantern to light their way.

For Kronecker this introduction to the Tasman area whetted his appetite for further climbing, and he set his sights on the possibility of ascending a virgin peak. He decided to return up the Tasman Glacier, with Fyfe and Clark as his guides, to attempt a climb of Mt Darwin, the high attractive rock pyramid which divides the Tasman and Darwin Glaciers. They left the Hermitage on 18 March 1894 en route to Ball Hut and De la Beche bivouac. There was a lot of freshly fallen snow on the mountain and Fyfe was anxious to climb it only under good conditions. However, as the weather was improving, Fyfe suggested they should take advantage of it and attempt the ascent of the beautiful Glacier Peak, which at that time was thought to be a 10,000 foot mountain.

Situated on the Main Divide, it presents a fine snow and ice climb on the upper sections with a steep clearly defined ridge leading down the eastern flank. Almost devoid of rock features, it stands in stark relief to Mt Douglas, an adjacent rock peak. While the approach to this peak from the Fox Glacier névé on the western side of the Main Divide is more straightforward, the eastern flanks of the mountain rear up very steeply from the Tasman Glacier and are strewn with rotten rock ridges and cascading icefalls. Nevertheless, it seemed possible that a route existed opposite the De la Beche bivouac, and Fyfe decided it was worth a try.

They left at daylight on 20 March 1894, but starting so late in the day and with the last vestiges of summer beginning to disappear, their chances of success were lessened. Crossing the Rudolf Glacier, Fyfe led unerringly up the hitherto untried rock ridges and snow slopes. At first the angle was easy but after two hours and at 6,000 feet the rock became steeper and they roped up. The loose shingle of the lower rocks gave way to firmer holds as the rock got steeper. Shortly the ridge ran out and Fyfe was faced with a hundred feet of quite demanding rock before cresting the rise and leading onto a snowy dome where some steep step cutting was required.

They reached the top of this projection at 11.30 am, only to find that Glacier Peak still rose airily before them on the Main Divide some 1,300 feet higher. Unfortunately the area now separating them from it was interlaced with many large crevasses and bergschrunds. They had actually climbed an outlying peak which is an individual feature on the mountain landscape. With Glacier Peak in sight they decided to keep going, but in another hundred yards found their way cut off by an ice wall. It also became apparent that the ascent of the peak would require some 500 feet of steep rock climbing at its base. Faced with these difficulties, and the limitations of some members of the party, and the lateness of the hour, they turned to make their descent. Later Tom Fyfe expressed the view that the climb of Glacier Peak

would best be done via Emas Dome as they had, but from there further to the north to proceed up the avalanche gullies until the north-east ridge was gained. This turned out to be the route later used by H.E.L. Porter and his guide, Vic Williams, in 1930 when they made the first ascent from the Tasman Glacier. The route Tom Fyfe's party had been on was not completed until 1950 when it was climbed by W. Beaven and F. Gibbs.

Guides and tourists on the upper Tasman Glacier in 1896. Left to right: Jack Clark, Mrs and Mr Maxwell, Mr Mahler, Tom Fyfe, Dr Kronecker.
Source: Kinsey Collection, Canterbury Museum.

Fyfe's attempt was a typically pioneering one, full of unexpected difficulties. On their descent they improved their route, taking the northern spur instead of the complex southern one used on the ascent. Dropping quickly down to the glacier, they reached the bivouac at nightfall, thus completing the first attempt on any of the Main Divide peaks in this area. Although they had not reached the top they had explored a rugged and hitherto unvisited section of the alpine chain. (To this corner of the Southern Alps Tom Fyfe later returned with Malcolm Ross in 1897, making a successful ascent of Mt Haidinger.)

The ascent of Malte Brun and the views gained from the summit had given Fyfe an opportunity to study possible approaches to neighbouring mountains. One of these was Mt Darwin. This peak lies some distance to the north of Malte Brun and stands out as one of the major peaks in the Tasman Valley. Like the others in the area it was unclimbed. The day after their attempt on Glacier Peak they moved camp across the Tasman Glacier to the base of Malte Brun near where Malte Brun Hut was later built in 1898. This was an easy day and provided well-earned rest after the rigours of the previous day. They camped in pleasant surroundings amid tussock and scrub, collecting the firewood for their camp.

The weather was beautifully fine and the views all around were magnificent. The massive icefalls and glaciers which flow 6,000 feet down the eastern side of the Minarets seemed to hang, layer upon layer, like a gigantic curtain falling in folds to the valley below, occasionally snapping off to form avalanches which thundered and spilled their way to the glacier, finally spreading out in an elegant fan shape. Kronecker noted that the night 'was very bright with a charming full moon spreading a magic splendour over the icy surroundings'.[11] The fresh snow on the rock having melted during the fine spell, Fyfe was satisfied the climb could be attempted.

Taking advantage of the brilliant full moon, they were ready to start at 2 am. They moved out onto the Tasman Glacier away from the big crevasses which flank the sides and onto the easier going in the middle. As is to be expected on pioneering expeditions, there was some uncertainty as to the best route to follow. They walked up the glacier until they reached the first snowfield that descends from Mt Darwin's long west ridge above Darwin corner. In two hours they had climbed to about 6,000 feet, but found their way barred by a heavily crevassed area. They had already had to climb down one bergschrund and up the other side, so when daylight arrived at 5.30 am they crossed to rocks at their first opportunity. Using a convenient rock chimney, they then made good progress and after crossing more bergschrunds, Fyfe led them out onto the prominent west ridge. This stepped away towards the summit and Fyfe hoped that if they followed this it might prove an easy path. But rock ridges are seldom as they seem, and this one is cut by a hundred-foot gap. He

100

circumvented this obstacle by dropping down below it onto snow until, at 11 am, after more mixed snow and rock climbing, they gained another high point 800 feet above.

They had now been moving continuously for nine hours and the strain was beginning to tell. Kronecker said that at this point: '...very much exhausted I was nearly turning around and leaving the ascent unfinished'.[12] However, after a rest and encouragement from both Fyfe and Clark he revived, and the three men set off for Darwin's final peak which rose 500 feet higher to the north-east. Here, with steep drops on both sides of the ridge, they cut steps in the ice and again up the last section, finally reaching the highest of Mt Darwin's numerous summits at 1 pm. The view was all-encompassing, with unclimbed peaks stretching north, west and south. To mark the occasion and the spot, they built a cairn and placed their names in a bottle, doubtless with great satisfaction.

After thirty minutes on the summit they turned away, facing a long descent. Time was now of the essence if they were to reach the Tasman Glacier before dark. The descent was not easy, and at one point Kronecker lost his footing on the ice but was held on the rope by the two guides. Having chosen a slightly different route of descent, they had to do a lot of downhill step cutting that was sometimes difficult and time consuming. Eventually an easier route was found, and further down they were able to avoid the bergschrunds and so by nightfall they were once again out on the Tasman Glacier. Here they had a short stop and waited for the moon to rise, the second occasion on this climb that they had travelled by moonlight.

By 9 pm all three were back at their Malte Brun camp tired and hungry, having eaten their last scrap of food at 3 pm during the descent. Kronecker and Clark decided to sleep there, but Fyfe, rather than turn in supperless, set off immediately for the Hermitage. After travelling down the Tasman, he stopped for three hours' sleep at Ball Hut at midnight before leaving at 3 am and he reached the hotel in the morning in time for breakfast. The whole trip says something about his endurance — and perhaps his appetite.

Jack Clark, Temuka-born, and only eighteen years old at this

time, had had a taste of the high peaks while he was working at
Glentanner Station. 'My first visit in the heart of the alpine
region was in 1893 when I accompanied Tom Fyfe on a photography expedition to a saddle on the arête of De la Beche. On that
occasion we reached an altitude of 7,000 feet and took pictures
of the Malte Brun Range.'[13] During the following winter, to get
more experience, he made a solo ascent of the peak at the head
of Lake Wakatipu, Mt Earnslaw (9308 ft), a feat which has
seldom been featured in mountaineering histories. Noted for
both his steady nerve and his affability, Jack Clark later became
an excellent guide and did much to induct Peter Graham into the
art and science of mountaineering.

By the end of March 1894 Tom Fyfe had been climbing in the Mt
Cook area for over three months. He then returned to Timaru,
having undertaken at considerable expense the most sustained
period of high alpine climbing done by anyone in New Zealand
to that date. During that short time he had attempted Mt Cook
with George Mannering and Marmaduke Dixon, and with
George Graham he had pioneered Fyfe's Pass to the West Coast
and climbed The Footstool and Mt De la Beche. He had also
ascended Malte Brun solo and had guided clients on climbs of
Mt Darwin, Glacier Peak and Hochstetter Dome. All but the
attempt on Mt Cook and the ascent of Hochstetter Dome were
new climbs. It was on this experience that he drew, four years on
from his first alpine climbing, when he returned to the Hermitage in the 1894-95 season to try again to climb Mt Cook.

1. T. C. Fyfe, "The First Ascent of Malte Brun," *NZAJ* Vol. 1, No. 5,
    (May 1894): 258-262.
2. A. Anderson, taped interview with the author, 12 May 1985.
3. P. Graham, "T. C. Fyfe: In Memoriam," *NZAJ* Vol. 15, (June 1953):
    287.
4. Malcolm Fyfe, taped interview with the author, May 1984.
5. T. C. Fyfe, May 1894.
6. Ibid.
7. Ibid.
9. Ibid.
10. C. J. Maxwell, "The Ascent of Hochstetter Dome," *NZAJ* Vol. 1, No.
    6, (October 1894): 341-350.
11. F. Kronecker, "First Ascent of Mt Darwin," *NZAJ* Vol. 1, No. 5, (May
    1894): 265-268.
12. Ibid.
13. *Weekly Press*, 16 May 1895.

8

MT COOK— A PEAK TOO FAR

Every colossus of nature inspires awe. Mt Cook is no exception, whether viewed in the crimson of a West Coast sunset or seen from the east at closer range. A phalanx of precipitous faces and ridges rises to form a summit a mile long, made up of three interconnecting peaks at an average height of 12,000 feet. It rears up as a massive upturned wedge of ice and rock culminating in the finely balanced encounter between earth and sky that is the summit ridge. Below its glaciers brown mountain tussock is interspersed by the remnants of the primeval beech forest. Although the mountain is wholly on the eastern side of the Main Divide, it is so dominant that with Mt Tasman, Mt Sefton and Elie de Beaumont it reigns supreme over the lowland forests of South Westland. To any mountaineer Mt Cook presents a magnificent challenge.

Non-climbing visitors to the Hermitage, unless they avail themselves of a tourist flight, often see only the mountain's South Face rising to the Low Peak. There are, however, other sides to the peak that are of special interest. On its western slopes, the ice and rock of the Hooker Face lead naturally up to the Middle Peak, and beyond the Hooker Face lie Earle's Ridge, the Sheila Face and the North Ridge. All these approaches require a combination of excellent rock and ice climbing skills. On the eastern side of the peak are further difficult routes where technically exacting standards are demanded of climbers who attempt the cavernous Caroline Face, the steeply sloping East Face or the high curving ice of the East Ridge which separates the two.

The problems with the north-eastern route attempted by Green in 1882 were that it was very long, it was threatened by avalanches and it required sustained periods of step cutting. This approach, using a camp on the Haast Ridge and then up the Linda Glacier, was the route used by Mannering and Dixon in their attempt on Mt Cook in 1890, and by Dixon, Mannering and

Fyfe in November 1893. During the two summer climbing seasons, 1891-92 and 1892-93, Mannering and Dixon had suspended their pilgrimages to the area, and had not attempted the peak. Dixon was keenly aware that Fyfe and Malcolm Ross were capable of making it to the top, and he was aware too of overseas interest, particularly the plans of the English climber, Edward Fitzgerald.

Meanwhile Tom Fyfe's interest in mountaineering had become the major focus of his life. With his father's success in business he was able to indulge his new-found sport. From Timaru Fyfe travelled regularly to Mt Cook using the family horse and trap. Still young and single, he could save enough to support himself for several months' climbing and he also earned money as a guide at the Hermitage. So at a time when few people had either the time, the money or the inclination for mountaineering, Fyfe had organised his affairs so as to be able to climb each summer.

During the 1893-94 season Fyfe had climbed extensively elsewhere throughout the region because he had agreed that he would stay off Mt Cook. Dixon had made Fyfe promise to avoid Green's route for two years unless he and Mannering were included. But Dixon was worried, writing that 'it became evident that decided action was necessary for we could not "tapu" our peak against other New Zealand climbers in Fitzgerald's company'.[1]

When in 1894 news arrived of Fitzgerald's plan to scale unclimbed peaks in New Zealand with the famous Zurbriggen as his guide, Dixon advanced plans that he had already made. For him, besides personal ambition, national pride was at stake. He wanted Mt Cook to be climbed by a party of New Zealand mountaineers rather than see that prize fall to an English climber and his Swiss guide. Of his attitude to the latter prospect, he wrote that 'one of our honest defeats is worth a dozen guide climbs'.[2] Jack Adamson at the Hermitage showed the same attitude, offering Dixon all the assistance he could muster, so that 'a cockney would not climb it first'.[3]

Fyfe had doubts about the chances of success using Green's

104

route in 1894, but his agreement with Dixon virtually limited him to it at that time. Underlying the relationship between Dixon and Fyfe there was intense competition which surfaced on occasion. However, when Dixon heard of Fitzgerald's expedition, he telegraphed both Tom Fyfe and Malcolm Ross to ready themselves for a November attempt. Fyfe did not favour that idea so early in the season, so he did not agree to join the climbing party, and his place was taken by Kenneth Ross, brother of Malcolm. The latter wrote that Dixon had 'no fewer than seven refusals from climbers who had at one time or another expressed their willingness to join him'.[4] When Malcolm and Kenneth Ross arrived at the Timaru railway station on 5 November 1894 they were met by Tom Fyfe and Jack Adamson of the Hermitage. In an attempt to dissuade Malcolm Ross they raised doubts about the possibility of climbing Mt Cook at that time, adding that the Hermitage would be unable to supply provisions. However, the Ross brothers departed for Mt Cook and met Dixon.

The three men established a high camp on the Haast Ridge and Dixon cut steps up to Glacier Dome. The weather was poor, however, and they withdrew to dry out at the Ball Hut. In the intervening five days Tom Fyfe and George Graham clearly had had second thoughts. Dixon wrote that much to the surprise of the three climbers at the hut, as the day of 10 November ended they 'were roused by a further noise outside... Presently however the door opened and in walked three men with ice axes, Alpine rope and other climbing paraphernalia'.[5] It was Tom Fyfe, George Graham and a runholder named Matheson, who was keen to see what the Tasman Glacier was like. After some discussion of plans it was agreed that they would combine their efforts and resources and try to climb Mt Cook together. Matheson apart, it was a strong and experienced party, and it had two exceptionally good rock climbers in Fyfe and Kenneth Ross. The latter was a seaman and thus well used to rope work, heights and rough weather conditions. Matheson also agreed to accompany them to the summit on this his first trip to the glacier, and so the ever resourceful Dixon 'nailed up his boots with hobs and clinkers for the ice-work'.[6]

For the next twenty-two days, from 17 November to 8 December 1894, the party made a series of attempts on the mountain — first trying to place a camp on the ice plateau, and then trying to climb the peak. During this time they actually set out from their high camp on four occasions with serious intentions of reaching the summit. Their only permanent shelter was at Ball Hut and it was a long way from the Haast Ridge. The distances they had to travel and the altitude they gained and then lost each time bad weather threatened, called on all their reserves of energy and commitment. Four times they had to evacuate the camp and retreat to Ball Hut from the Haast Ridge or beyond, and each time they had to bring with them their tent, which was in such poor condition that it leaked.

Over this difficult period other problems strained the party further. There was a continual shortage of food: Fyfe, in addition to his climbing to and from the ice plateau, made two separate journeys to the Hermitage and back for extra supplies. In the high camp none of the party slept well — except for George Graham — and this made them tired and sometimes irritable. Such conditions militated against their chances of success — as did the length of the route they chose to follow. The party also lacked internal cohesion, and personal ambitions to be the first to climb Mt Cook were not far beneath the surface.

At 6 am on the morning of 16 November 1894 four men — Marmaduke Dixon, Tom Fyfe, George Graham and Kenneth Ross — began their assault on Mt Cook. By then Malcolm Ross had used up all the time he had available and, accompanied by Matheson, he departed for Timaru. Between times Matheson had been useful, helping to recover swags thrown down the Haast Ridge, and augmenting the food supply by killing a kea with his ice axe. By the morning of the 18th, again using skis brought up for the purpose, Fyfe, Graham and Ross, with Dixon in the lead, were navigating through fog towards the peak, but they could not be sure exactly where they were and returned to camp. At 11.30 that night Fyfe began cooking a meal that was deemed to be breakfast in readiness for another attempt. By 1.30 am they were leaving for the peak, giving themselves every opportunity of success with an early start.

Fyfe took the lead, and by lantern light he piloted the party

Skis are used to stay the tent in this first high camp on the Grand Plateau in one of the 1894 attempts on Mt Cook.
Photo: Malcolm Ross.

through the heavily crevassed area of the Linda Glacier. After five hours of difficult progress they halted to adjust their clothing and boots and to focus their minds. Dawn had broken, and the mountain was lit up like a firework by the rays of the sun rising over Malte Brun.

Because it was still early in the season snow conditions were difficult, and with the skis now discarded because of the steepness they made slow progress, sometimes in thigh-deep snow. However, by eight o'clock they had climbed to a point high on the glacier and the route ahead looked prone to avalanche danger. Here they stopped for a snack and some discussion of plans and the best approach to take. When there is a divergence of opinion about the best route to follow, parties of four often split into teams of two, each following a different route, and if one is found not to be practicable that party usually retrace their steps to the point where they split from the other one, and follow instead in their path. On snow climbs they often catch them

107

quickly, not having to make steps. When they rejoin they are fresh and can take over the snow plugging when their companions tire.

When the party took its well-earned rest at dawn, Fyfe questioned the safety of the route stretching ahead. He said he thought it was menaced by the ice cliffs above and he felt that the objective danger was too high to continue on it. Dixon says that 'I had myself formed the same conclusion when passing here with Mannering in 1890'.[7] Kenneth Ross later wrote that Dixon and he held firm in favour of continuing up Green's route on the basis that it had been climbed before and that it would be wasting time and a good day to attempt to find any other approach. The alternative was Fyfe's idea of climbing up the rock face towards the North-East (Bowie) Ridge, a route that Fyfe said would lead to the summit and which he told them he would 'guarantee to take us up'.[8] He also argued that the route he envisaged would be a more meritorious way to climb Mt Cook because it had not been attempted before.

His opinion was strongly held, and instead of splitting into two parties the others concurred, and at around eight o'clock Fyfe led off up steep rock towards the Bowie Ridge. With a drop of 2,000 feet below them, they negotiated a small snow couloir and carried on climbing. Kenneth Ross described the scene: 'One man moving at a time, while the others kept a good anchorage with their axes, we climbed the last bit of the snow slope and the first rock work was begun. Fyfe taking the lead, did not keep us waiting; in fact I had not been more than five minutes in his company on the rocks before I came to the conclusion that he was exceptionally good at rock work, apparently being capable of detecting the safest and slightest foothold or hand-grip with wonderful rapidity.'[9]

The climbing was at a sharp angle, and Dixon said Fyfe kept encouraging them onwards with optimistic comments such as 'the peak in sight', and 'it's an interesting climb'. However, with a party of four on such steep rock, their progress was slow. Fyfe got frequent questions from the men behind as to how it looked, to which he replied that they could be assured that 'it looked much easier'.[10] Dixon said, though, that the easy part never seemed to get nearer. Fyfe revelled in the quality of the climbing, but after six hours a major obstacle reared above them in the form of a massive rock wall, very steeply angled, beyond the top of which they could not see. Again each climber had a look at the problem and gave an opinion on the feasibility of the route. Kenneth Ross recalled that: 'Fyfe declared he could get up, but might not, he thought, be able to come down again.'[11] The general conclusion reached was that they should try a different approach, climb back and try to get back on to Green's route at a lower point.

They did this but lost a lot of time, and it was five o'clock in the afternoon before they got back to their initial route. Their intention was to try to complete the climb by moonlight and by 6.30 pm they were at 10,500 feet. But there was a lot of step cutting ahead and still 2,000 feet to climb, and when the temperature dropped to -6° Fahrenheit, the cold became too intense for their tweed clothing to keep them warm enough. It was too cold to risk standing out all night, and they resigned themselves to defeat. By 10.30 pm they were back at their camp, determined to try again but also considering how lucky it was they had not been hit on the descent by a large serac weighing several tons that had fallen close to them.

There followed a day of light snow that made climbing out of the question and they returned to Ball Hut. Fyfe departed for the Hermitage on foot to get more food while the others looked for and found their swags abandoned earlier on the Haast Ridge. They were also pleased to find that Jack Clark had tried to get up to the plateau the previous day to climb with them but had been held back by thick fog, and as he had been returning to the Hermitage he had thoughtfully stopped at Ball Hut and there left new supplies of food for them. When Fyfe eventually returned with enough provisions to continue their attempts, they departed again for the ice plateau. They were slightly amused to be told by him that down at the Hermitage Jack Adamson had been concerned for their safety because of the difficult weather conditions, their lack of food and the time they had been away, and that he had put plans in readiness for mounting a search party.

Fyfe had actually met Adamson on his way up to look for them when he was going to the Hermitage to get more food and was told of this.

On Sunday 25 November the same quartet turned to face the long haul again — Fyfe's fourth attempt and Dixon's seventh. They climbed back up to the camp. Kenneth Ross's description captures the atmosphere: 'Intending to make an early start and not being able to sleep owing to the cold frosty air, we lay chatting, singing and discussing the possibility of our success on the morrow, while Fyfe, to retain as near as possible the normal heat of his body, burnt a candle under his blankets. About 9.30 pm the lamp was lit, and a kettle of snow put on so that we might have a good substantial meal before leaving, as we had been economising as much as possible — our two previous meals that day consisted principally of porridge and a little meat minus bread. About 12 o'clock (midnight) we crept out of the tent, one man staying inside to pack all the spare clothing, etc, into a sleeping bag, and to pass out such articles as we required, while the others set to work to unfasten the ski and ice axes that were holding up the tent. At 1 am we were roped together ready for another attack upon the ice-walled fort of Aorangi.'[12]

Seven o'clock saw them advancing high into the Linda Glacier and they quickly reached Green's Rocks where the step cutting up into the snow couloirs awaited. A hard frost ensured that they had no alarms from falling ice, and after a second breakfast and photography by Ross and Fyfe it was time to recommence the ascent. The lantern, no longer required for the ascent, was left at Green's Rocks. They began cutting steps in the ice. During the climbing that followed, Kenneth Ross made a serious mistake: he placed his ice axe on an ice-covered rock — from which it quickly slid away to the depths below. Now one ice axe short for the next eight to nine hours, they set to work cutting hundreds of steps up the mountain, Fyfe and Ross doing it in the morning and Dixon and Graham later on. Having no crampons, they had to fashion each step carefully in the ice to prevent any chance of a fall.

By the late afternoon the whack and whirl of the axes saw them closing fast on the final icecap and bergschrund. But the length of the route again began to take its toll. Dixon wrote: 'The time was 5.30 pm, and I remarked to Fyfe "I do not think we shall reach the top tonight".'[13] Fyfe agreed with him. Ross now borrowed Dixon's axe, and then Graham relieved Fyfe, taking the step cutting in hand and making the ice fly down in showers. He took them quickly onto the ridge that runs up to the summit. The angle had eased back to an easy thirty degrees. With the virgin summit perhaps less than an hour away and the technical difficulties not great, the only question that remained was whether the peak could be climbed at this late hour without the party spending a night out. They had cut up another eighty feet when Fyfe, ever mindful of the dangers of becoming benighted, called a halt, saying to Graham, 'We had better turn back'.[14]

Turn back they did, with Ross and Graham acceding to Fyfe and Dixon's experience. All his life Kenneth Ross regretted this decision, as both he and Graham were going strongly for the peak.[15] The decision made, they descended carefully and reached the end of the difficult section just as the last vestiges of daylight were vanishing. Here they lit the lamp and Fyfe led them through the maze of crevasses by its light. In another three hours they were back at their camp on the plateau, too tired from such a long climb to even contemplate discussing future plans or the events of the day. In the intense cold all but one of the party had a sleepless night. Dixon wrote that 'Graham has the happy knack of sleeping under any difficulties and was much envied by us all — while Fyfe and I did not get one hour's sleep in five nights spent in ski camp.'

The next morning began with a debate which brought to the surface the competition in the group to be the first to top the peak. When there had been food enough for all four climbers to stay in the camp they could all attempt the climb. Now there were only a few scraps left. Fyfe broached the idea that he and Kenneth Ross should attempt the peak again while Dixon and Graham carried the camp down to Ball Hut. Dixon was not in agreement and proposed that they draw lots as to who should go down to the hut for fresh supplies, but even this, he says, 'was not agreed to'.[16] Clearly no one wanted to be fetching more supplies while the others might claim the glory of the first

ascent. The issue found its resolution in an impersonal quarter
— the weather. Fyfe called Dixon outside the tent, where they
were met with an angry sky of clouds all round in black and
white streaks and a lack of wind which was foreboding. They
agreed that a storm was imminent. The die was cast: they must
now descend from their camp with all possible speed.

This was the third time they had climbed well up on the icecap
of Mt Cook only to find there was too little time to complete the
climb. Perhaps in Fyfe's mind when he had urged turning back
was the memory of the difficult night Green had had in 1882
when he stood out on the mountain with his guides. Also, the
group had left, thousands of feet below, the lantern with which
they had intended to light the way when darkness fell.

Later Ross and Dixon each wrote that they thought it had been a
mistake to turn and that they could have climbed to the summit.
Ross's chagrin is understandable, since he and Graham had
obviously felt they were close to getting to the summit and also
because they had not been involved in the decision to turn back.
Dixon's disappointment at his seventh bid is understandable
also: together with the nearly successful attempt in 1890 with
Mannering, he had now been within sight of the summit twice.
Whatever the regrets, the decision to turn back was probably a
wise one. The party had managed without Ross's ice axe, but its
loss might have been serious had they stayed longer. Fyfe had
remained firm that the risks of benightedness were too great, a
view he was to maintain throughout his climbing career. With
the grey dawn the next morning there came a violent storm: if
they had remained on the mountain it could well have brought
disaster.

They packed their swags and broke camp immediately, and it
almost became each man for himself. Now in a great hurry to
descend to even lower levels, Fyfe went ahead of his companions. Ross wrote that as the storm began to whip up the snow,
Fyfe took only his camera and a few odds and ends and started
to descend. Assuming that the others could manage, he moved at
great speed away down the mountainside, seemingly oblivious
to any difficulties they might face in having to pack the tent with

the storm blowing. Graham and Ross took the remaining items from inside, leaving Dixon with the now frozen tent. With great difficulty Dixon lurched along and soon was reduced to climbing up the Glacier Dome on hands and knees. George Graham went back to help him, and together with Ross the three followed Fyfe who was by then well down the Haast Ridge en route to Ball Hut. With the snow flying and visibility difficult on the Haast Ridge, Kenneth Ross became totally exhausted and asked to be left in a camp on his own. Dixon and Graham would not leave him, and together they were forced to sit out the storm that night, in extreme cold and with very little sleep.

They had good cause to envy their climbing mate as they shivered in their tent, expecting that in the meantime he had reached the security of Ball Hut, having carried a light load and descended in the lee of the Haast Ridge. Fyfe certainly felt remorse. Ross recounted that Fyfe 'upbraided himself a good deal for having left us'. When the storm abated in the morning he returned up the glacier to look for them, not knowing whether they would be dead or alive. Ross says, perhaps with some irony, 'His heart was in his mouth as he wended his way up the Tasman Spur, and saw at the bottom of the couloir the swags [which Dixon, Ross and Graham had pushed off ahead of them] but no sign of climbers. He was actually afraid for a time to go near them. He expected to get some clue by closer examination; but when he reached them, he could not tell from the shoulder straps whether they had been sent down intentionally or not.'[17] The three benighted climbers soon descended, however, sliding down the 2,00 foot couloir towards their swags, and it was much to Fyfe's relief that he saw them eventually coming down towards him. All were now safe, but one wonders what the three others thought when Fyfe told to them how the wall of Ball Hut had been blown in three inches by the storm.

The group's best efforts had not been good enough to reach the summit. Now Kenneth Ross had to return to work, and Dixon planned to do the same. Fyfe remained at the Hermitage intending to explore with George Graham an entirely different approach to Mt Cook via the Hooker Glacier. When Dixon got to Timaru, however, he arranged yet another attempt, this time with Dr Norman Cox, and returned to the Hermitage with him. Fyfe, in keeping with his undertaking, delayed his plans to explore the Hooker approach and together with George Graham he set off with Dixon and Cox for his fifth attempt to climb the mountain. It was to be what is now called an alpine-style attempt — a forty-hour climb from Ball Hut, making no camps, and thus carrying no tents, blankets or other weighty equipment. Organised in a hurry, it indicated once again the strength of Dixon's desire to succeed on Mt Cook.

They left the hut at 11 am on Saturday 8 December 1894 and climbed steadily that afternoon and, by the light of the moon, into the night. By 4 am on Sunday morning they had reached the head of the Linda Glacier and were only about 1200 feet below the summit, when they were met by a wind that chilled them to the bone. Fyfe now put it to a vote whether to continue, and with Graham and Cox opted to retreat, thinking from the appearance of the clouds that a storm was brewing. Dixon reluctantly agreed and they returned to Ball Hut. As fate would have it, for the next twenty-four hours the weather remained fine, thus dashing the best chance of success that any party had had up to that time. Dixon was furious at the outcome, believing that the party had been too hasty in its decision.

Three days later in a newspaper he said as much, suggesting that his ambitions had been undermined by the cautious attitude of Fyfe and his companions and that they had not put their hearts into the climb. Divisions within the party now came into the open. Dixon's erstwhile climbing companions were shocked at Dixon's outburst, but confined themselves to corresponding privately with him. Cox went so far as to attribute the failure to Dixon himself, describing him as selfish and unsympathetic. In reply, Dixon termed that an 'aggravating insult', adding that there were 'only two ways to deal with it — either come down and do my best to punch your head in or give you a straight tip or two'.[18] Coming from the secretary of the New Zealand Alpine Club, that reply was too much for Cox, and he resigned his membership forthwith.

It is clear that Fyfe was just as keen to climb the mountain as were Dixon, Mannering, Graham and the Ross brothers, but it is also clear he wanted to climb it according to the standards of safety accepted at the time. This meant retreating when bad weather threatened. He was also prepared against his own wishes to limit his choice of route to that determined by Green, Dixon and Mannering, respecting the efforts they had previously made.

However, success on the mountain using a completely new route, he believed, would not only achieve what had not up till then been possible but would do so more meritoriously. Dixon's withdrawal from the struggle left Fyfe free to explore different approaches to the mountain with honour satisfied, having kept his part of the undertaking.

The Fyfe-Dixon agreement meant so much to Dixon that he made it clear that if Fyfe broke it, he would claim a share of the glory. Before he departed from the Mt Cook area about 11 December, he left a note for Fyfe at Glentanner Station which said: 'If you climb Mt Cook in our steps I shall certainly reserve to the party the credit of the ascent … and my tip is to let Malcolm Ross describe it in the [Alpine] Journal.' He also suggested to Fyfe that there is 'not the slightest hurry … I do not think Fitzgerald has any intention towards Cook'.[19]

Unconvinced, Fyfe now set about a detailed exploration of the Hooker Glacier to find a new route to the top of Mt Cook. The possibility of this more direct approach had been suggested by Roberts in his survey, and the saddle at the head of the Hooker Glacier had been reached by Harper and Blakiston in 1890. Harper believed that a route seemed feasible from that area. The mountain itself on this whole western side remained untrodden, and on his return to the Hermitage Fyfe set about trying to find out whether 'a practical way to the summit might be found from the upper part of the Hooker Glacier'.[20]

To assess that possibility he made three more climbs. The first was a reconnaissance to the head of the glacier with Jack Adamson, the second an attempt to reach the higher summit via the Middle Peak of Mt Cook with George Graham, and the third and finally successful one was an ascent out of the glacier up a narrow couloir now known as Fyfe's Route and then up a steep rock climb of the North Ridge.

Fyfe wrote little about his mountaineering, but as his account of these latter two climbs is precise and interesting and is not easily available, it is appropriate to describe the first complete ascent of Mt Cook as he wrote it a few weeks later.

1. Dixon, "The Attempts on Aorangi from the Eastern Side," p. 8.
2. Ibid.
3. J. Adamson, letter, 29 June.1894, M. J. Dixon papers, Canterbury Museum.
4. M. Ross, *A Climber in New Zealand,* p. 53.
5. Ibid.,p. 69.
6. Ibid., p. 71.
7. Dixon, p. 11.
8. Ross, p. 81.
9. Ibid.
10. Ibid., p. 82.
11. Ibid., pp. 82-3.
12. Ibid., p. 93.
13. Dixon, p. 14.
14. Ibid.
15. Author's interview with A. Anderson.
16. Dixon, p. 15.
17. Ross, p. 103.
18. M. J. Dixon, letter to N. Cox, R. D. Dick papers, Canterbury Museum.
19. M. J. Dixon, diary, Canterbury Museum.
20. *Otago Daily Times,* 21 February 1895.

9

SUCCESS — AND CONTROVERSY

On 21 February 1895 under the heading 'First complete ascent of Mt Cook', Fyfe's account appeared in the *Otago Daily Times*, the newspaper which had employed Malcolm Ross. Except for the beginning, which summarises previous attempts, it is reproduced here verbatim, using Fyfe's spelling. (He spells Clark as 'Clarke', as many others have done, but until 1900 Jack Clark signed his letters without the additional 'e'.)

* * * *

Though most of the preceding climbers had followed closely in Green's route, and Green himself had been dissuaded by Dr Von Haast from trying for a route on the Hooker side, I held to the opinion that a practical way to the summit might be found from the upper part of the Hooker Glacier.

Accordingly, on the morning of December 11, about a month after our arrival at Mount Cook, Adamson (of the Hermitage) and I left for a preliminary exploration of the Hooker side of the mountain. Having nothing but a camera and a little food to carry, we romped along quickly, reaching the first icefall by 9 am. We had some little difficulty in crossing several of the crevasses — one, which had fallen in, we descended into and cut steps up the opposite lip; but greater difficulty was experienced in crossing the debris of an avalanche which had apparently fallen from the Empress Glacier. To walk erect was impossible, and our only means of progress was by crawling on all fours — very trying sort of work.

The bergschrund below Harper's Saddle was reached and crossed by 2 pm, and then an hour's laborious step cutting up an extremely steep ice-slope — hand-holes having to be cut in places — brought us out by the crest of the ridge some 100ft higher than the actual saddle. This saddle, 8,500ft above sea level, was first 'done' by A.P. Harper — the first secretary of the New Zealand Alpine Club — after whom it is named. It leads over on to the La Perouse Glacier, one of the principal feeders of the Cook River, flowing into the West Coast.

On our way up I had eagerly scanned the mountain and had picked out two possible routes whereby I thought the summit of Aorangi might be reached. The more feasible way viewed from Harper's Saddle appeared to be to reach the western spur of the lowest or most southerly peak, and then from that point to follow along the ridge over the middle peak, and thus up to the top of the highest peak. The other route, and the one by which we ultimately reached the top, was to keep up the Hooker Glacier to its termination, up a nasty-looking couloir to what has been called Green's Saddle, on the great Tasman arête, and then to follow the ridge of the latter to the summit. The greatest difficulty of this route appeared to be a large 'bergschrund' at the head of the glacier. Bergschrunds are great chasms in the ice, which usually occur at the head of snowfields. Besides being of great width — often from 30ft to 40ft — they are made much more formidable by the upper lip standing much higher than the other, with heavy overhanging caves. Snow-bridges often form across the fissures, by which they may be crossed; but, failing these, they are sometimes insurmountable.

We had not sufficient time to reach this point and investigate, so I there and then decided to first try the western spur of the lowest peak, and after making a few exposures with the camera we started homewards at 3.30 pm. We were very hungry; and alas! we had eaten all our supplies. Never shall I forget the joy I experienced on finding the bone of a fowl which I had picked and thrown away coming up, but now was content to suck all the way home! The hotel, after a long, broiling day, was reached some time past midnight. Our faces were terribly burnt with the sun. So painful were they that even to smile was impossible, and any would-be joker was immediately silenced in a most effective if not an altogether playful manner.

On December 16 Graham and I left the Hermitage late in the afternoon, and, keeping along the Hooker track for six miles, camped on the left of Fairbank's creek. This place — which as a camping ground was all that one could desire — we afterwards made our headquarters. A light nor'wester had been blowing all day, and as the sun set it increased and brought much rain. The rain continued to fall at intervals next day, and, as being cooped up in a 7x5 tent with nothing to do but smoke is not very conducive to good spirits, we grew ill-natured and growled at everything. Graham went out several times, and vented his pent-up feelings in vain efforts to murder a solitary kea, which, wheeling round in circles screeched so derisively at him that he vowed he would devote the rest of his life to the extermination of the species.

The morning of the 18th broke fine, and as we watched the mists gradually rise higher and higher, revealing the peaks of first one and then another giant mountain, our spirits began to rise wonderfully also. To be even alive on such a morning at such a place gives one a feeling of happiness and contentment dear to all lovers of nature.

We decided to spend that day reconnoitring, and leaving camp at 9 pm we kept along the lateral moraine for about a quarter of a mile before turning to the glacier. Expecting to find the cre-vasses of the Hooker much worse than they were on our first reconnoitring expedition, we carried along some branches of scrub, intending to leave them bit by bit to mark the best route. The first ice-fall brought us to difficulties; snow-bridges by which Adamson and I had crossed were entirely gone, and the crevasses were all much more open.

This Hooker Glacier breaks up very early in the season, and the great number of longitudinal and transverse crevasses which intersect and form square-topped towers of ice called seracs makes it very difficult to get over. After two hours' threading in and out we got through the worst icefall, and then the glacier was comparatively easy walking. Reaching a point directly opposite Baker's Saddle, we turned off from the main glacier on to a long snow-slope lying between the Empress and Noelline Glaciers.

What we most desired was to find a suitable place for a bivouac at as high an elevation as possible, and with this object in view we directed our steps towards the top end of a rib of rocks, the height of which was about 6,500ft. Reaching this, we found that the top was covered with small scree or stones, and would, with a little levelling, afford us some shelter for a night. It was still early in the day, so, after a short rest, we ascended for another hour to get a better view of the upper snow-fields of the Empress Glacier coming down from Mount Cook. We could from our standpoint see almost the whole route, and concluded that the only doubtful part was the upper rocks under the first peak.

Our descent to the Hooker Glacier was delightfully rapid and pleasant. The snow being in perfect condition, we glissaded the whole way, shooting scores of small crevasses in great style. This glissading or shooting down a snow slope is very exhilarating, and sometimes slopes that have cost hours of hard work in step-cutting coming up may be descended in a few minutes. On our way down the Hooker Glacier we agreed to explore the right side for a better route. Some avalanche debris from the Moorhouse Range that choked up the fissures on that side was tempting, but the line of route was dangerous on account of the likelihood of a fall occurring at any moment. However, we found that we could pass so quickly over the dangerous part that the risk was reduced to a minimum, and we always afterwards used this route. We reached Fairbank's creek at 6 pm, and after a refreshing dip in its cold waters (its temperatures generally being under 38° F) we were soon fast asleep on our luxurious couch of snow-grass.

Our programme now was to bivouac on the rib of rock we had chosen, and then the following day make our assault on the peak. The weather was so settled next day that we decided to do without a tent, and, each taking a blanket and food sufficient for two days, we reached our bivouac at 4.30 pm. Whilst Graham boiled the billy I levelled off a spot about 6ft by 4ft. This was sheltered on one side by a large rock, and we protected it on the other by building a break-wind. The surroundings of this our second bivouac were wonderfully grand and impressive. As I lay snugly wrapped in my blanket I could just see the topmost tip of Aorangi peeping over a rugged spur, appearing in its immaculate purity against the deep blue sky like a bit of cloud. Then St

David's Dome, with its soft, beautiful curves, formed quite a contrast to Mount Stokes, from whose precipitous sides the avalanches never ceased to fall. Immediately below us, and stretched away up to the very summit of Aorangi, lay the Empress Glacier, a picture of which the eye never tired. Falling over an almost perpendicular wall of rock it joins the Hooker — a wonderful mass of serac ice — which, lit by the departing sun, showed the most exquisite colours imaginable.

I was early astir, being as usual unable to sleep on the small stones, and had the fire blazing at 1.30 am. Heating some soup and making tea I hustled Graham out of the blankets, and as the night was beautifully mild (34° F) we sat in perfect enjoyment at our early breakfast. The first streaks of dawn appeared at 2.45, and hastily roping we started off in the dim light up the steps we had broken two days previously. Keeping a little above where we had turned on that occasion, we passed through a gap in the spur onto the névé slopes of the Empress Glacier. After crossing a crevasse on a rather frail snow-bridge, we had several more to negotiate before reaching a long slope lying between the true western spur and an offshoot which runs in a more northerly direction. The snow was very hard, and steps had to be chipped with the axe. Nearing the termination of this slope we took to the spur, thinking it would be quicker and that we should avoid some nasty-looking cracks running right across from side to side. The arête became so bad and irregular that we were soon forced to take the slope again. On coming to its head some slight difficulty was experienced in finding a place to get on to the spur; but, once gained, it proved good, and for about 500ft an easy grade. After this it became much steeper and gradually narrowed in to a sharp ridge. After some 2,000ft of rock climbing the lowest peak came in sight, and at 10.30 am we stood on the true western arête running up to the same. We had now the choice of cutting steps up on to the crest of the arête or, by keeping down a little on the northern side, of skirting along the rocks. We chose the latter, and found that, although owing to their being partly buried in snow they were difficult, still they were much easier and quicker than step cutting. We had now been in the sun some time, and a short halt was cried for 'tucker'. Vain efforts were made by one of the party to melt some snow, but even the sultry language he indulged in had no effect on its icy coldness. It is a strange sensation this, being surrounded by snow and ice, and, though 'dying' for a drink, unable to obtain a mouthful. Skirting along these partly buried rocks, and cutting a few steps here and there across slippery patches, nothing stopped us, and at 11 am we stood on the highest rocks. We were now at an altitude of 11,700ft, and our prospects of doing the remaining 600 odd feet looked 'rosy'.

From here it was necessary to descend about 400ft to reach the saddle which separates the first and second peaks. This we had little difficulty in doing, good rocks running right down. The sun was now very powerful, and we took advantage of it to melt the snow and drink to our hearts' content. Step-cutting commenced at a couloir which runs from the Empress Glacier right up to this col, and the axe was kept steadily going until the summit of the middle peak was reached. On nearing the crest of the arête we soon had ample evidence that it was heavily corniced, the axe going right through when we were several feet from the edge. It may be here explained that a cornice is a great eave of snow which projects over a mountain ridge, and is due to the action of the wind. Cornices are most treacherous, and have to be avoided at any cost. Keeping, therefore, about 20ft away from the true crest, we cut steps along the face of the ice-cap, thus practically making a long traverse. At 1 pm we stood on the top of the second peak, only 176ft lower than the actual summit of the mountain. A glance and we saw that our chances of doing the remainder were remote. Although only so little in actual height above us, it was still a long way off, and the arête was so corniced, and took so many turns, that to 'do' the summit would require a long traverse involving many hours' work.

Having the other route to fall back on, we decided not to expend our energies further on this one, and so again calmly accepted defeat. The view from the second or middle peak was exceeding grand, and it would be presumptuous for me to attempt any description. Imagine river and lake, bush and plain, sea and sky, all blended together and forming one vast panoramic picture, and some faint conception may be had of this entrancing view. Although we had not attained the topmost tip of Aorangi we

The High Peak of Mt Cook, first seen by Tom Fyfe and George Graham from the Middle Peak in December 1894. On that occasion they were prevented from reaching the High Peak because of the corniced ridge in the foreground and the step cutting required.

Photo: Nick Groves, Hedgehog House.

certainly had discovered an easy and, more important still, a safe route to the second highest point of the Southern Alps.

Shortly after 2 pm we started the descent and carefully going down the steps cut in the clear blue ice, soon regained the rocks. Stopping for some food on the highest rocks just below the lowest peak, Graham seized the opportunity to build a cairn, leaving a bottle in the centre. The descent down the rocks was very slow and tiresome, and it was 5 pm before we struck the long snow slope. The snow was now in grand order, and we took

123

The High Peak of
Mt Cook as it is
now, following the
collapse on the East
Face in 1992.
Photo: Nick Groves,
Hedgehog House.

full advantage of it by glissading almost all the rest of the way to
the bivouac. The only stops that were necessary were when
crossing some specially wide crevasse, or in making a traverse to
get in a good uncrevassed line. Where the slopes were not steep
enough plunging through the snow was the order of the day, and
woe betide the man coming last on the rope if he made a false
step, for he would immediately receive a jerk from his companion which, completely upsetting him, made him take an invol-
untary header into the snow. I have a vivid recollection of
Graham's legs waving in mute supplication whilst he vainly

tried to extricate his head and shoulders. All the smaller crevasses were shot glissading. Whilst shooting one the rope somehow became entangled, and pulled one of the party up with a jerk just as he got fairly across the fissure, his feet resting on one edge and the back of his neck on the other. He was quite equal to the occasion, however, for stiffening himself, he lay with perfect composure until assisted by his companion.

The bivouac was reached without further incident at 6 pm, and hastily packing up our blankets, we glissaded to the glacier below. The bad icefall was quickly negotiated, and striking a bee-line across the glacier, Fairbank's creek camp was reached at 8.30 pm. The weather had been perfect all day, but it now commenced to rain, and there was every appearance of rough weather, so that we decided to find our way down to the Hermitage that night. The track down is difficult enough to follow even in daylight, but by the feeble light of a candle requires infinite patience. We arrived at the Hermitage about 1 am, and after 21 hours' constant going we were only too glad to turn into a comfortable bed. In our last expedition we were fortunate in being joined by young Clarke, from the Hermitage, who had climbed with us last season, and whose enthusiasm gave new life to the whole affair. Leaving the hotel with six days' supplies, we made our first camp on the evening of the 22nd December, and got everything snug. Next day we toiled, painfully swag-laden, through the ever-widening crevasses to a second bivouac farther up the glacier, narrowly escaping a fall of rocks that came bounding from the Moorhouse Range. We arrived sore and tired, although the actual distance covered and height gained were trifling. Little inclined as we were for another day's swagging, 10 am next day found us again wearily plodding on our upward course. We pitched the tent under the lee of a huge block of ice that had apparently fallen from St David's Dome at a height of about 8,000ft. An arch was cut into this block, a break-wind built around, and so sheltered were we that I believe we could have weathered a severe storm. Leaving Clarke in camp, Graham and I proceeded up the glacier with the double object of breaking steps and of exploring the large bergschrund at its head. We kept to the true right of the glacier going up, but found it very much crevassed and swept by avalanches from St David's Dome and Mount Hector. We passed some enormous crevasses. Some we estimated as being fully 200ft across and of great depth. Another uncommon thing so high was a vertical shaft descending into the glacier. Graham anchoring, I crawled to its edge and peered down, but could see no bottom, its blue sides shading away until lost in impenetrable darkness.

Two hours brought us to the bergschrund, and our worst fears were fully confirmed. No bridge of any description spanned its gaping depths. Our only chance was to find a passage where it ran out against the rock face of Aorangi. Traversing to this we saw that it was possible to descend right into the bergschrund and reach the rocks at its end. These looked barely practicable. We kept to the left side of the glacier going back, and found it much simpler, only one crevasse of any consequence having to be dealt with. Our bleak bivouac was regained just as the sun sank behind Mount Stokes. After some food and a refreshing drink of hot tea we lay down on our icy-cold couch, fondly hoping to snatch a few hours' sleep. Vain hope! On going to rest at these high camps the usual plan is not to undress but to crowd on everything obtainable, and anyone leaving an article of cloth-ing lying about is sometimes greatly surprised at the mysterious manner in which it disappears at night, but always religiously turns up again in the morning in time to be rolled into the owner's swag.

At 2 am Graham, shivering and growling, arose to prepare breakfast. We had brought a good supply of dry firewood from our first camp, and breakfast was ready much too soon for Clarke and I, who were making the most of the blankets. Getting on our boots with great difficulty — they being turned, apparently, into something akin to cast iron — we packed up everything we were likely to require, and, roping together, moved upwards at 3.15 am. The snow was very hard, but the steps we had broken the previous day were of great assistance, and an hour's climbing saw us standing on the lower lip of the bergschrund. Letting out the rope to its full length, one of the party descended into the bergschrund and squirmed along the ledge of rocks as far as the rope

would reach. Then the others crossed on to the rocks. Cling-ing as we were to a narrow ledge, with scarcely any hand or foothold, and with an almost perpendicular drop into the chasm below, our position was far from enviable; and, as the leader slowly and with great difficulty made his way up-ward, a slip seemed, to say the least, not altogether improb-able. Some snow laying on the ledge had to be shifted, and caused a little delay, and for 40 minutes the excitement and suspense were too intense to be pleasant. However, we managed to get across in safety. Above we found the snow hard, and we kept well against the rocks for handholds. This slope gradually converges into a deep ravine formed by the frowning crags of Aorangi on the one side and by Mount Hector on the other. Beginning at Green's Saddle and run-ning out in the slope just above the bergschrund, a rib of rocks divides this ravine into two narrow ice-filled couloirs. As we got higher up the amount of snow lying on the slope became less and less, and at last the clear blue ice was reached. Cutting steps across a little branch couloir, we decided to cross the couloir lying between us and the rib of

The western approaches to Mt Cook as seen from the summit of Mt La Perouse, showing, left to right, High, Middle and Low Peaks. The North Ridge, the route taken by Fyfe, Clark and Graham, runs towards the High Peak from the end of Fyfe's Route, which climbs 2000 feet from the Hooker Glacier.
Photo: Colin Monteath, Hedgehog House.

rocks, and to endeavour to keep along its ridge. At first these rocks proved difficult, a rotten slaty rock having to be dealt with, but they improved towards their top end. As we neared Green's Saddle the arête of these rocks became very sharp, with precipitous sides, and in two places was capped with ice. We had to cut steps up these places, and without further bother reached a point a few feet below Green's Saddle at 8 am. Here we were stopped by a break in the rib which completely barred direct access to the saddle. Turning a little to the left, we climbed up over what was perhaps the worst rock of the whole ascent, on to the southern arête of Hector, and from thence descended to the saddle. The arête which runs from here to the summit of Aorangi is, with the exception of one slaty stratum, composed of good, sound rocks. This slaty stratum, about 30ft in height, was most difficult. Half-way up, the leading man got into difficulties, all holds being just beyond his reach, causing him to make an awkward traverse by hand-holds only to a little chimney, up which he writhed his way. Above this, the going was good, and we rapidly rose. Looking back at 10.30 am, we could see that we were far above all the surrounding peaks, and, although the top of Aorangi could not be seen, we knew it could not be far distant. One wall of slate brought us to a standstill, and we had to descend a few feet, leave the ridge, and work our way around the obstacle. The wind was now piercingly cold and we were glad to muffle our faces in anything to protect them. A few minutes' respite from its bitter blast and a slight snack were now very acceptable, and we climbed down to shelter on the sunny side. What with consulting maps and sketching, the 'few minutes' were pro-longed into an hour and a half, and it was just midday as we filed off upwards. At 12.30 the slope of the arête became easier, and shortly afterwards the final top appeared about 400ft above us.

I am afraid that the reckless way in which we romped over those last rocks was very foolhardy, but one would indeed need to be phlegmatic not to get a little excited on such an occasion. The slope of the final icecap was easy and only required about 100 steps, which were quickly cut, and at 1.30 on Christmas Day we exultantly stepped on to the highest pinnacle of the monarch of the Southern Alps.

Three principal arêtes meet at the summit. The angles of two of them, the southern and northern, are fairly steep right to the summit. The other, the Tasman arête, is an easy grade. The actual top consists of a sharp ridge sloping quickly north and south, a precipice on the eastern side, and a crescent-shaped ice-cap running from the western side. Westward, our view was somewhat marred by clouds, but beyond the clouds the coast line, especially towards the north, could be seen stretching mile after mile. Eastwards, owing no doubt to the great heat, there was a haze through which we could just discern the ocean. South-wards, towards the coast, we saw a very high peak which we took to be Mount Aspiring. Turning northwards we looked into the very heart of the Southern Alps. Range after range, and peak after peak in wild confusion impressed one with an almost overpowering sense of desolation and solitude. A phenomenon which, as far as I can remember, has seldom previously been noticed in New Zealand, was the curvi-linear dirtbands extend-ing across the Tasman Glacier, which from this height were clearly visible. A short stay of 20 minutes only was made on the summit, and then leaving an old sugar bag spread on the icecap, with the idea of seeing it afterwards from the Sealy Range with the aid of a glass, we started off downwards. The first rocks were soon reached, and here we portioned out the remainder of our food. We also built a cairn, leaving a tin on which Graham scratched our names and the date.

We left these rocks at 2 pm, and kept closely to the way by which we ascended. We soon came to the steeper rocks. Now came the real climbing. The last man on these rock descents has much the worst of it. In bad places he must anchor and assist the others down. Green's Saddle was passed by 5.20 and just as we got a few feet below, a large avalanche of rocks shot playfully past, making the very mountain tremble as they ricochetted from crag to crag down the mountain side, fragments, as when a shell bursts, leaping up. Going down the slaty rocks near the couloir, Graham made a slight slip, and making a grasp to maintain his balance dropped his axe into one of the narrow couloirs. Down,

down it slid, until at last it was luckily arrested by a lump of snow just on the edge of a crevasse. At first we could see nothing but to cut steps down to it — a longish job — but afterwards thought of a plan whereby that labour might be avoided. Fixing the rope to a sound rock and letting it out to its full length, Graham lowered himself 100ft and just managed to grasp his axe. His performances coming up, if not altogether graceful, were at least amusing.

This delayed us the better part of an hour — a delay that we could ill afford, as it would soon be dark. When nearing the bergschrund an ominous, not-to-be-mistaken whiz above warned us that danger was coming. Crouching close in to the rock, several pieces of stone went pinging over us at a pace that rendered them invisible and buried themselves feet deep in the soft snow. This particular place is in my estimation the only dangerous part of the whole route, but fortunately only so in the afternoon. All the way down I had been anxious to get across the bergschrund before dark, and, but for the dropping of Graham's axe, we would have done so. It was with great uneasiness I saw that we should have to stand out all night or risk climbing down in the dark. The latter was preferred. Too dark to see either hand or foot-holds, our senses of touch was all we had to rely on. One at a time we moved on, the other two endeavouring to anchor; but, judging from the holds that I myself could obtain, a slip by one would have 'done for' us all. However, the schrund was left behind, and with it the greatest difficulties of the descent. Now for the first time we gravely congratulated each other on the ascent and descent of Mount Cook.

We reached the bivouac tired and wet, only to find that one side of our snow break-wind had fallen on to the tent and, melting, had soaked everything. It was very cold, and it is not all joy pitching a tent with the thermometer down to about 28deg. We turned in supperless: no one volunteered to face the cold and melt some snow. So cold did we become that at last we were forced to burn a candle in a tin can underneath the blankets, while the hours of darkness passed wearily away. Day dawned at last, and, hastily packing up, we plunged away down the glacier. We reached our first camp at 7 am, and were glad to rest till

The summit trio — left to right, Jack Clark, George Graham and Tom Fyfe photographed shortly after their successful climb on Mt Cook on Christmas Day, 1894
Source: Unknown

10.30, meanwhile basking in the sun and making great inroads into a bag of oatmeal. As we lay, idly watching the north-west cloud swirling overhead, our trials were all forgotten and I regretfully thought — there is but one Aorangi.[1]

* * * * * * * *

News of the success spread quickly, and it was widely acclaimed. Praise was given not only because the peak had been climbed by a completely new route — a very difficult one, it should be emphasised, and one that was not followed for another fifty years —but also because the honour had been achieved by New Zealanders. Fyfe was characteristically modest, being reported in the *Timaru Herald* as saying that '... they were very fortunate in regard to weather, and found the ice in splendid order, favourable circumstances that may not attend future expeditions.'[2] The newspaper said that 'much satisfaction is felt here at Mr Fyfe being so exceedingly successful'.[3] It also reported that Fyfe and Graham would join Fitzgerald's party on the way to Mt Cook, but those negotiations fell through.

Dixon's near successes on the mountain were now overshadowed and he could not conceal his disappointment. The unpleasant exchanges by letter with Cox in December 1894 were

131

echoed in a letter that Dixon wrote to the *Weekly Press* on 11 January 1895 which belittled the achievement of Fyfe, Graham and Clark:

... The very name of Mt Cook is so hackneyed, and it is so shorn of its glories from a climbing point of view by Mr Green, and the ice staircases which exist cut as to the very ice-cap by his followers that Mr Fitzgerald will regard it only like walking up a high road to follow Mr Green's route, and may think it worth his while to find a new route up from the west or Hooker side. So well known and so simple is Mr Green's route that it is quite possible Mt Cook will be climbed by ladies in the near future: it is simply a matter of good luck in finding the crevasses, the snow and the weather all in travelling order at the same time ...[4]

This drew a reply over the pseudonym Mountaineer.

Sir, — The deprecatory remarks of Mr M. J. Dixon regarding the ascent of Mount Cook by Fyfe, Graham and Clark come with very ill grace from the Secretary of the New Zealand Alpine Club. Mr Dixon refers to Mount Cook being 'shorn of its glories from a climbing point of view by Mr Green'. Evidently Mr Dixon did not think this, as he continued year after year with Mannering to strive for the honour of reaching its summit, and even after Fyfe had climbed with him and Mannering last year he made Fyfe promise that he would not set foot on the mountain for two years unless he (Dixon) were in the party! This hardly looks as if Mr Dixon thought Mount Cook 'shorn of its glories from a climbing point of view!' Neither would one judge this to be his opinion when, on receipt of the news that an Englishman was coming out with guides, Mr Dixon hurriedly arranged a party to make the ascent last November. But now the peak has been climbed evidently it is a case of 'sour grapes' with Mr Dixon.

Mr Dixon also refers to 'the ice staircases which exist, cut on to the very ice-caps by his (Mr Green's) followers', and adds, 'Mr Fitzgerald will regard it only like walking up a high road to follow Mr Green's route, and may think it worth his while to find a new route up from the west or Hooker side'. Well, when Mr Fyfe's account appears in due course, it will be seen that this is actually what Fyfe and party have done, so that Mr Dixon may

132

have saved himself the trouble of writing about 'a high road to the summit of Mt Cook.' The idea that the ice staircases exist is all bunkum, as any mountaineer knows that such must have disappeared long ago, and can exist only in the vivid imagination of Mr Dixon. As to ladies climbing Mt Cook — perhaps they will, and then it will be proved that they can do what Mr Dixon has been trying for years, but has failed to accomplish. I prefer, however, to take the estimate of men like Mr Green and Kaufmann in preference to that of Mr Dixon. They say that the ascent of Mount Cook by Green's route must at all times be regarded as a difficult and dangerous undertaking. It pains me to have to write thus, but I feel that injustice is being done, and cannot remain silent.

Mr Dixon refers to Clark as a new man, but, as a matter of fact, he has a much better record than Mr Dixon — Mount Darwin, Hochstetter Dome, Glacier Peak (partial ascent), Earnslaw (ascent alone), and now Mount Cook. How many peaks of this class, or indeed of any importance at all, has Mr Dixon topped? None!

There are other wild statements in what Mr Dixon has written, but I have no wish to take up too much of the space of so well-conducted a journal as the Press *and, in conclusion, I would simple recommend him in future to be a little more generous and to give 'honour to whom honour is due'.— Yours etc. Mountaineer.[5]*

The bitterness continued on 31 January 1895 with Dixon's reply to Mountaineer:

Sir , — If your correspondents signing themselves 'Mountaineer' had had the grace to sign their names, they might prove to be Timaru men, and possibly men whom, amongst others, I endeavoured to include in a New Zealand party, with the object of climbing to the actual summit of Mount Cook, before the Englishman came. And it is most unworthy of a man — who, pretending to be a 'mountaineer', to make a number of cowardly personal remarks and then not to have confidence enough in his opinion to sign them. Possibly if he had signed them he would have got 'salted' — but he prefers to put on a mask and stab in the dark.

133

Mount Cook was to all intents climbed by Mr Green and afterwards by Mannering and myself, and so accurately did Mr Green describe the route, and so well do we know every inch of it, that it is like going up a high road, and is purely a matter of good luck as to weather, &c, and Mr Fyfe knows this quite well.

Perhaps 'Mountaineer' in his ignorance does not know that the 'so-called' years Mannering and I have spent 'climbing Mount Cook', do not amount, when every day is counted, to the time spent on Mount Cook by Messrs Fyfe and Graham this summer, and a ten-days' Bank holiday does not allow of spending half the summer on Mount Cook. Steps cut in hard ice remain a long time in spite of everything, but I'm not prepared to prove that any trace of our steps yet remain on Green's route. As to the 'deprecatory remarks of Mr M.J. Dixon regarding the ascent of Mount Cook', 'Great is Diana', and so I might continue to cry, but I am not going into rhapsodies of fulsome admiration of Mr Fyfe, and I do not think he expects it, and if Mr Mountaineer could only see a little more clearly through those remarks he would see that they attribute great credit to the independence of judgment and character of Messrs Fyfe and Graham. Messrs Harper and Adamson concluded years ago that Mount Cook could be climbed from the Hooker, although they did not actually 'point out' the route as I inadvertently put it in the Press, *January 4th; and as to Jack Clark, I only took Fyfe's word for it, 'that he was a beginner and anxious to learn', and as to making Fyfe promise 'after' he and I and Mannering had tried Mount Cook in 1893, 'that he would not set foot on Mount Cook for two years', 'Mountaineer' is wrong, as Green's route was specified, and the Hooker side was open to Mr Fyfe all last summer, when most of his time was spent on the glacier, and the compact was made 'before' our 1893 climb, not after. In this whole affair I strove for one point, and that was that a New Zealand party should first 'top' Mount Cook, and I did succeed, though personally had little to do with it.*

Perhaps 'Mountaineer' will in future try to get at the merits of the case before making a cowardly attack on a comrade by means of an inappropriate, assumed name.
Yours, etc., M. J. Dixon.[6]

Dixon's reaction annoyed the climbers who had been with him

in the attempts on Mt Cook in the previous month. Cox, writing to Dixon, told him that Fyfe was 'boiling over with indignation at another slight to him'.[7] Thus, public and private rancour and mistrust overtook the competitiveness and individual ambitions which underlay the friendships, partnerships and agreements among a number of climbers. Perhaps the value attached to the achievement had been too high to expect that the result would be otherwise.

Dixon was impulsive in his first comments about the failure of his party and then about the success of another party by a new route. His disappointment was understandable: no one else had had the first ascent of Mt Cook so clearly in their sights for over five years or had come so close to success so often. He had a New Zealander's pride in his wish to see the prized peak fall to a local rather than a visitor. Although his chagrin did not allow him to acknowledge this immediately, within a few months he had published a balanced account of attempts on the mountain. A summing up of Dixon as a climber must recognise his positive attributes and his contribution to mountaineering. He was a moving force in the early years of the New Zealand Alpine Club and in 1893 was elected to membership of the Alpine Club in London. In the mountains he was innovative, courageous and determined, adding strength to the parties he climbed with. It is fitting that overlooking the Haast Ridge, the first stage in his several assaults on Mt Cook, there stands a fine peak named Mt Dixon.

Fyfe had achieved his own ambition and doubtless that of many other climbers of the time. He had also achieved another ambition — to succeed on a route other than Green's, believing that it would be more meritorious to do so. Furthermore he had done so not only quickly and safely but on a route that was difficult — one that continues to demand nerve and skill from today's mountaineers. Few people reach such standards. His success on our highest mountain is attributable to his personal skills as a climber on both ice and rock, to his extensive climbing and guiding experience, to his assessment of Graham and Clark as companions and to his judgement of risks.

If Fyfe had retired from alpine climbing at the end of 1894, his achievements on Mt Cook and elsewhere would still have warranted recognition of him as the outstanding mountaineer of his day in New Zealand. Yet over the next twenty years new challenges beckoned, and he continued to make his mark in the Southern Alps.

1.   *Otago Daily Times*, 21 February 1895.
2.   *Timaru Herald,* 4 January 1895.
3.   Ibid.
4.   *Weekly Press,* 11 January 1895.
5.   Ibid., 24 January 1895.
6.   Ibid., 31 January 1895.
7.   N. Cox, letter to M. J. Dixon. R. D. Dick papers. Canterbury Museum.

10

CLIMBING IN FIORDLAND

Following his success on Mt Cook, Fyfe returned to Timaru where he met Fitzgerald and Zurbriggen whom he had beaten to the prize. He could afford to be magnanimous towards them. As they were leaving Timaru for Mt Cook he joked to Zurbriggen, 'I hope you will leave us a few peaks to do.' To this the serious Swiss replied, 'Oh no, we come out to climb mountains, we climb all we can.'[1] Using crampons and often assisted by Jack Clark, the two visitors accomplished a good deal, making first ascents of Mts Sefton, Tasman and Haidinger, climbing Mt Sealy and making the first crossing of the Copland Pass. Because New Zealanders had beaten Fitzgerald to Mt Cook, he refused to try it — he is said to have remarked that he had been pipped at the post, and by 'a damned tinker'. However, in March 1895 Zurbriggen, accompanied part of the way by Jack Adamson, climbed Mt Cook by another new route. Thus by the end of the climbing season of 1894-95, New Zealand's mountaineering history had been marked by a number of notable achievements.

These two ascents of Mt Cook shifted the focus off that peak — it was not climbed again for another nine years — and some of the Canterbury climbers who had been involved in attempts on it began to pursue other interests. Fyfe, however, remained active both as a private mountaineer and then as a guide at the Hermitage. His next climbing ventures were materially assisted because of his friendship with Malcolm Ross. In the 1890s new photographic and printing techniques made it possible to produce illustrated magazines, and resorts such as Rotorua, Milford and Lake Wakatipu were favourite subjects. The government was beginning to promote tourism, and it was fortunate for Tom Fyfe that his friend Malcolm Ross was able to combine his journalistic skills with his climbing interests, to the benefit of both of them. Having close contact with the Liberal government, Ross was paid for producing feature articles about New Zealand's alpine areas, and between 1895 and 1898 this arrangement in effect subsidised

Fyfe and Ross in climbing and exploration in various places — at first, further south.

Easter 1895 saw Fyfe and Ross in Queenstown, heading for two peaks in the Remarkables Range overlooking Lake Wakatipu. They had planned to sleep out and save themselves the walk from Queenstown before climbing, but when a storm blew up in the night they opted to stay at Eichardts Hotel. This left them a long walk to the base of the climb. Thinking it would not be a snow climb at that time of the year, they again discarded their ice axes and boots in favour of the rubber-soled shoes Fyfe had found so useful on Malte Brun the previous season. However, the initial climbing was a snow plod which in their poor state of fitness required frequent rests. The day was cold and cloudy and they interrupted their progress with occasional drinks from a bottle of spirits. But even thus fortified, they found that climbing rock in freshly fallen snow was no easy matter, and on the steep ridges of the Remarkables they had to take great care. As the clouds began to lift they became keenly aware of the depths beneath them, and on the Queenstown side they encountered very steep rock.

Forced to climb around some steep rock towers rather than go over the top, they found it difficult to negotiate the solid ice without an ice axe to chip out holds. Ross wrote: 'Fyfe at last got stuck at a place that seemed absolutely perpendicular. The rocks were glazed, there were few if any grips for twenty or thirty feet … and if we slipped we might go down a thousand feet, or, for all we could tell, five thousand. We roped up.'[2] With time passing quickly, they picked their way carefully up the remaining pinnacles and eventually saw through a gap in the clouds the beautiful Lake Alta to their left. This lies nestled above the present skifield that has now made this area easily accessible. Despite the cold and their lack of fitness, they enjoyed their attempt on this striking range of peaks. Climbing on mixed snow and rock was Fyfe's forte, but with the cold numbing their bones and the highest summit still some distance off, they decided to turn back. They made a speedy descent to lower levels by way of snow glissades and scree slopes. Just as night fell they reached the ferry at the Kawarau River crossing, where the woman in

charge gave them some milk and her boy ferried them across the river in the boat.

That climbing was but a pipe-opener for an expedition to Fiordland a few weeks later, their objective the unclimbed Mt Tutoko. In fact in 1895 Fiordland was virtually all virgin territory, Mitre Peak being the only summit that had even been attempted. The only climbing of any significance in the region had been William Quill's solo climb in 1890 up the difficult and dangerous face beside the Sutherland Falls, 1904 feet high. The following year in another solo effort he had tragically met his death trying to find a route across the Gertrude Saddle to Milford Sound.

The climbing party that assembled at the township of Te Anau in May 1895 was a strong one, among them Tom Fyfe from Timaru and three Dunedin men, Kenneth and Malcolm Ross and William Hodgkins, a lawyer. A climbing expedition so late in the year, however, ran the risk of fickle weather. It had been

Kenneth Ross, left, and Harry Birley, together with Malcolm Ross, who took this photograph, ascended the highest peak on The Remarkables above Queenstown in the 1890s. Their summit flag is limp in the calm air. Birley also climbed Mt Earnslaw (9,308 ft) solo on its first ascent on 16 March 1890.
Source: Malcolm Ross, Canterbury Museum

139

William Quill,
surveyor, who
made three ascents
of the Sutherland
Falls.
Photo: S. Quill

intended to sail from Wellington to Milford Sound aboard the government steamer *Hinemoa* with cabins generously placed at their disposal, but bad weather in the north delayed the ship on its voyage south. The party travelled instead to the head of Lake Te Anau in a small steamer which made slow progress pointing into the head wind on the lake. Ross said: '...the supply of fuel would suddenly come to an end, but this was a matter easily remedied, for they simply ran the nose of the vessel ashore, and the captain and engineer, with the passengers assisting, plied the axe in the forest primeval until a new supply of fuel had been put on board.'[3] At the landing point they set out in the direction of Mackinnon Pass, laden with vast amounts of supplies.

Already there was a good deal of newly fallen snow on the peaks and in the valleys, and they found that there was some heavy plodding to be done. The views they enjoyed on their arrival at the pass, however, fully compensated them for the effort of tramping with heavy swags. On the right rose the parapets of Mt Balloon, its granite sides mottled with the new snow that had fallen, and with its black walls offering little prospect of an ascent. As if balancing the view from the pass, Mt Elliot, its double summit protruding from the grey slabby side of the mountain, seemed grandly to survey the four invaders — those mere specks on the pass below. It was in this arena, high on the rocky ramparts of Mt Balloon, that Tom Fyfe was to have one of his few narrow escapes in his many years of climbing.

The weather stayed fine, and he and Malcolm Ross set out to attempt the first ascent of Mt Balloon. This fine rock peak offered the type of challenge that Fyfe found difficult to refuse. Leaving the others on the pass, they headed directly towards the rock precipices that rose beyond the snow couloir that fell to the pass. Their first taste of mountaineering in that region presented some problems even for such accomplished climbers. Zigzagging up the rock which rose steeply above them, they tried to reach a ridge which ran up from Roaring Creek, and in doing so they made reasonable progress. A wall of over a thousand feet now towered high above them, but being granite rather than

140

Tom Fyfe (standing, upper left) and Malcolm Ross (sitting, third from left) are in this party in May 1895, en route to climbing in Fiordland.
Photo: Burton Bros, Dunedin

greywacke or schist, it offered good friction and hand-holds, especially compared with the loose fractured rock in the Mt Cook area.

However, as the autumn sun rose higher, it began to thaw and melt the fresh snow, and water poured down on them. They were climbing unroped, confident in their own ability and taking different routes. Ross commented that 'the climbing was unlike anything we had previously experienced'.[4] When Fyfe got into a difficult couloir which required his total commitment, his ice axe became an impediment and he left it behind. They were continuing to climb through the intermittent snow bombardments, but it was only a matter of time before a much larger snow mass would fall on them.

It soon did so, and they decided it was time to retreat. It had become evident that the mountain was completely out of the question, so, still some distance from the summit, they turned and started downwards. Fyfe went down first, well aware of the likelihood of further snow and rockfall. Just as he was moving around the base of the first rock step above the saddle, a large rock fell from high up on the mountain and headed straight towards him. Ross let out a loud warning yell. With the quick reaction so typical of him, Fyfe took evasive action — this time the unusual one of prostrating himself with his heels up the

141

Donald Sutherland, pioneer of Milford, shown with a billhook used for bush slashing.
Source: Southland Museum

slope and his face hidden under his arms to protect his head. His luck held: the rock landed a yard or two away, burying itself in the snow. It had been a narrow escape.

A further attempt on Mt Balloon was foiled by bad weather, and the party then made its way down to Milford Sound where the weather had cleared and the mists had risen off the sound. Enjoying the hospitality of Donald Sutherland and his wife, the owners of the accommodation house, they began to sample the spectacular scenery of Milford in late autumn. Unfortunately for Fyfe he began to suffer badly from an attack of neuralgia, but remaining meanwhile with the party, he turned his hand to fishing on the sound. Hailing from South Canterbury where skill with rod and reel is widespread, he had some success. Balancing himself upright in the stern of the boat he became the envy of the group, landing four or five cod and tarakihi. After a pleasant evening dining on the catch around an open fire, they turned in for the night, with the best of Donald Sutherland's renowned yarns ringing in their ears.

Early next morning they set off in a leaky boat for an attempt on the mountain then called The Mitre but today familiar as Mitre Peak. On their earlier attempt Sutherland and the artist Samuel Moreton had gained only the lower peak. This second attempt on the peak turned into a long and difficult day, and by eight o'clock in the evening they had still not returned. It was not until the moon was well up that the quiet solitude near the accommodation house was broken by the splash of the oars on the still water of the sound. This climb too had been unsuccessful; Mitre Peak's summit remained untrodden.[5]

Fiordland's remote mountains were then and still are difficult climbs, but, having achieved a good level of fitness, Fyfe and Ross decided it was time to attempt their prime objective, Mt Tutoko, the highest peak in the area. The monarch of Fiordland at 9,042 feet, it rises with great distinction as a massive bulk from a low altitude. It stands astride deep valleys, abruptly radiating many steep ridges, and down its flanks cascade numerous hanging glaciers.

142

Donald Ross, the guide who conducted tourists over the Milford Track at that time, had plenty of bush experience, and he led them to their highest camp on the north branch of the Cleddau River. However, after only a few miles on the journey up the valley, Fyfe suffered a further severe attack of neuralgia. He had to return reluctantly to Milford and forego this opportunity to take part in the first serious alpine climbing attempted in Fiordland.

The remainder of the party, after a long hard day carrying swags in virgin forest, but captivated by the scenery that opened up to them, established a high camp. They had made only ten miles from Milford Sound. During the last mile, however, they had been able to see at the head of the valley 'a fine snow-clad mountain'. They believed it to be Mt Tutoko, although, writing in 1914, Malcolm Ross recorded his doubts: 'Nothing definite could be deduced as to its position as the maps could not be relied on, the position of the river being wrongly marked.'[6] Next day, after ascending some 2,000 feet up the glacier beyond the camp, they attained the high snow and ice plateau under the peak. When they began climbing up it they immediately found that the ice required step cutting, and that was their mode of progress for the next four hours. Because the climbing was steep and it was late in the year for mountaineering, it was sunset before they got near the summit. Kenneth Ross had led the major part of this climb, showing what a strong and ambitious climber he was — prepared to push on for the summit despite the failing light.

They got almost to the top of this high Fiordland peak, but they had to turn back, defeated by dusk and a high final pinnacle of ice-covered rock. They were nevertheless delighted by the alpine vista before them. Paramount among the array of peaks was one that Malcolm Ross described as 'a magnificent snow-clad mountain about 9,000 feet high, adjoining Tutoko to the west'. He named it Mt Fosbery and the body of ice which flowed from it the Age Glacier, after the Melbourne *Age* newspaper which partly sponsored the expedition. When they finally turned back, having read their aneroid at 9,000 feet, they believed they had only just missed climbing to the highest point of Mt Tutoko.

Hodgkins, writing in the *New Zealand Alpine Journal,* was quite sure they had, but doubts grew.[7] Later it was established that they had in fact been climbing a peak now called Mt Madeline.

Such were the difficulties for these first climbers in the alpine wilderness of Fiordland. The beauty and majesty of the area, however, made a lasting impression on Tom Fyfe. He agreed with Ross's appraisal of the views in the area embracing Mt Hart, Mt Balloon and particularly Mt Elliot, that they were as remarkable as might ever be gazed upon. He also warned later generations of visitors to Milford that 'the climbing is difficult owing to the dense scrub and the polished granite slopes and precipices on the mountains'.[8] The expedition, though unsuccessful, had opened up new possibilities, and other climbers began to seek the challenges of Fiordland summits.

Considering the enthusiasm of just a few years earlier, it is surprising that in 1896 the New Zealand Alpine Club based in Christchurch actually went into recess and was not fully reconstituted until 1921. (The centre of activity shifted from Christchurch to Dunedin, where a temporary revival occurred in 1914.) This absence of a formal organisation, together with the demise of the *New Zealand Alpine Club Journal,*[9] has sometimes given the impression that little mountaineering of any consequence occurred in the decade between 1895 and 1905.

The expedition led by Fyfe and Ross to Fiordland is just one example of the varied mountaineering activities that continued after the first ascents of Mt Cook. In 1897-98 W. G. Grave, Dr J. R. Don and A. C. Gifford also visited Fiordland. To get there, Graves cycled to Te Anau from Oamaru, and the party attempted to climb the real Mt Tutoko by what is now known as the Grave Couloir, but did not reach their objective.

Others were active elsewhere. The West Coast brothers, George and James Parks, continued their exploration of the Whitcombe valley. In 1898 in a journey lasting a month Jack MacKay and Jack Adamson made the first eastern crossing from the Hermitage to the glaciers of the Callery region and then to the West Coast. Zurbriggen came back to climb in New Zealand, this time

A. Talbot, left, and W.G. Grave, noted explorers of Fiordland. Talbot was a particularly gifted rock climber. Grave, a teacher in Oamaru, discovered the Grave-Talbot Pass in 1910.

as guide to an Italian count, Signor Borsolino. In this period Jack Clark continued his success as a climber, and he also had an influence which stretched for years ahead as a result of his having interested the young Peter Graham of Waiho in mountaineering. Clark also widened his climbing experience in Europe, becoming the first New Zealander to climb Mt Blanc. In 1900, with Herbert Butler of Australia, Jack MacKay again climbed from Malte Brun Hut into the Callery, in an another unsuccessful search for gold. In the same year Malcolm Ross ascended Mt Sealy. In January 1897 he and his wife, Forrest, had ascended the Hochstetter Dome, this being the first known instance of New Zealanders using crampons.

145

In May 1895 Fyfe returned from Fiordland to his parents' home in Timaru and resumed working for his uncle, James Craigie, in plumbing contracts throughout South Canterbury. He also began to court a young woman of Irish descent named Mary Ann Peake. During 1896 he worked in the North Island, and in June of that year he and Annie, as she was called, were married by Rev. Patterson in a Presbyterian church in Wellington. A year younger than Tom, Annie had been born in Hokitika, the daughter of Louisa and John Peake who lived in Revell Street. Possibly because John Peake was a publican, Annie did not condone alcohol, and so when Tom drank liquor it was away from home. She was not interested in the outdoors but accepted her husband's enthusiasm for mountaineering.

The winter of 1895 was one of the most severe recorded, and it probably kept all plumbers busy. With the spring thaw, however, there came the good news for climbers. On 11 September the government's policy of encouraging tourism led to its purchasing the Hermitage for £900. (Fyfe and Adamson had discussed purchasing it.) The building was in a run-down state, the company having lost £5,000 in the enterprise.

146

For Fyfe the change of ownership gave the hope of employment as a guide. But first the government had to decide on the management of the place. They tried to sell it as a leasehold venture, together with 42,000 acres of adjoining land which was part of the Birch Hill run. The conditions that were set attracted no offers, but while negotiations were going on during the summer season of 1895-96 the former managers, Jack Adamson and his wife, were designated as caretakers. They had larger responsibilities, however, and were expected to continue to provide a full hotel service to the public. Reports showed that that they did their best in difficult circumstances, but for some reason the decision about appointing a manager was delayed for months.

Eventually, on 7 September 1896, the manager and housekeeper of the nearby Glentanner station, Alexander Ross and his wife, were appointed to manage the Hermitage. Their instructions were to make these charges: 2s 6d for a meal or a bed, 10s a day for full board, and guide fees beyond three miles of the Hermitage of £1 a day. The costs of travel to the Hermitage, £4 10s per

Milford City, as Donald Sutherland's guest-house was known, from which Fyfe and his companions attempted Mitre Peak in May 1895.
Source: Canterbury Museum

147

Mattias Zurbriggen, left, and Jack Clark on the summit of Mt Haidinger, 8 February 1895. Edward Fitzgerald deleted Clark from this photograph when he published his book, but before leaving New Zealand he had given this copy to J.J. Kinsey.

Source: E.A. Fitzgerald photographs, Kinsey Collection, Canterbury Museum

person, meant that only people with some wealth could afford to visit. Adamson felt aggrieved at being overlooked in the new arrangement but his petition against it got nowhere.

Fyfe offered his services to the Department of Lands, writing: 'If there is any probability of the Government requiring a guide for the Hermitage I shall be most happy to offer my services. I may state as one who is very familiar with that district and its requirements that I am of the opinion that the Government should keep a guide there independent of anyone in the house — the charges are generally very high and the guiding poor and consequently tourists do not see half of what they would like to.'[10] He also mentioned his skills as a plumber as likely to be useful.

A. P. O'Callaghan, a departmental manager, wrote to the Commissioner of Crown Lands in Christchurch, praising Fyfe's attributes: 'Mr Fyfe is a young active man who has distinguished himself in climbing several of the high peaks during the past few years. He bears an excellent character, has a very intimate knowledge of the high range and would, I think, make an excellent guide if one should be required.'[11] Brodrick, the surveyor, also wrote in support: 'Mr Fyfe's qualifications are unexceptionable. He is the best man I know of to fill the position of guide at the Hermitage, and would be very handy about the place; he is a plumber by trade, but has done much mountaineering for the love if it. He was the first to ascend Mt Cook, has ascended many other large peaks and made a pass from the Mueller Glacier to the West Coast.'[12]

These testimonials made Tom Fyfe a strong applicant. In October 1896 he became the guide at the Hermitage, the first person appointed by the government with the sole responsibility of guiding climbers to the peaks and passes of the Mt Cook region. On 21 November 1896 Tom and Annie arrived, ready for Tom's full-time employment in the area he had made his own and which still contained many unclimbed peaks.

1. M. Ross, letter to J. J. Kinsey. Kinsey Papers. Canterbury Museum.
2. M. Ross, "Scrambles on the Remarkables," *NZAJ* Vol 2, No. 9, (May 1896): 159-172.
3. M. Ross, *A Climber in New Zealand,* p. 219.
4. Ibid., p. 225.
5. Ibid., p. 235.
6. Ibid.
7 W. J. Hodgkins, "The First Ascent of Mt Tutoko," *NZAJ* Vol. 2, No. 9, (May 1896): 172-180.
8. Ross, *A Climber in New Zealand,* p. 235.
9. Editorial and presidential letter, *NZAJ* Vol. 3 (March 1921): 3-8.
10. Department of Lands and Survey, S3041, Christchurch:National Archives, 21 September 1895.
11. Ibid.
12. Ibid.

11

GOVERNMENT GUIDE

Tom Fyfe's first job at the Hermitage was not to guide tourists but to make repairs to the building. It had become dilapidated and there was much to be done. He first covered the south wall with iron and made the whole exterior weatherproof, then varnished and painted, and replaced glass in broken window panes. He also saw to the surrounding area: more than twelve miles of walking and horse tracks in the area were newly constructed or reformed and upgraded.[1] The new managers set about refurbishment — muslin curtains for the twelve bedrooms, cretonne curtains for the dining room, and for the ladies' sitting room a couch and two easy chairs with cretonne coverings. They also asked for a billiard table and a piano for the entertainment of visitors. These facilities were needed as indoor recreation because in bad weather when they could not venture out, people often become bored and restless and were inclined to leave earlier than they had planned. During the early part of the season there was no regular coach service from the Fairlie railway terminus, but the road from Pukaki was improved and in January 1897 a bi-weekly coach service began which helped to encourage tourists.

Under Fyfe's supervision, work also began on a new hut further up the Tasman Glacier near Malte Brun. Of the view from the site, Fyfe declared in a report that 'it was the most extensive that could be obtained on the Canterbury side of the higher peaks of the Alps and the magnificent sunrise effects on Mount Cook could be seen to perfection. With the view to be seen across to the icefalls on the Minarets there would be few that could not be thus impressed'.[2] He was enthusiastic about the longer and more interesting glacier trips for visitors that could be offered through the new facility. It was named Brodrick Hut after the eminent surveyor who chose its site. The beautiful trip from Ball Hut up along the Tasman Glacier to the new hut became an alpine journey that many able-bodied tourists could accomplish.

150

The Fyfes had to negotiate with the Department about Tom's being paid for working on Sundays, about Annie's fare to the Hermitage and then about the cost of her accommodation. Board for both of them was settled at £1 4s per week, and with Tom being paid 10s for each day he worked, he could expect to earn up to £15 per month. These rates were fairly generous, especially when compared with the combined salaries of the managers of £5 per month, and might have caused some friction. Alexander Ross wrote to the Commissioner of Crown Lands in Christchurch on 30 November saying that 'The Hermitage Bush is on fire since Friday 27 November, it is not known how the fire started. Mr Fyfe was up on Thursday night about six o'clock, he was the only person up in the bush for the last fortnight.'[3] This could have implied that Tom Fyfe had started the fire, but there is no record of anyone taking the matter any further.

As the first full-time guide at the Hermitage, Fyfe had to establish a new and effective service. He welcomed visitors and described the facilities and the various trips available. For some a circuit of the Wakefield Track might suffice, but the more energetic and adventurous might want to go up onto the Sealy Range where on a clear day the beautiful tarns reflect the mountains beyond. For others a trip up to Ball Hut and onto the ice of the Tasman Glacier might have more appeal, the overnight stay in the hut adding to the feeling of remoteness from civilisation. In those days the glacier reached to a point near the hut and visitors could go to see the Hochstetter Icefall cascading from the Grand Plateau in its chaotic shapes. Some of those who ventured that far might be prepared to tackle one of the easier peaks nearby, such as Hochstetter Dome. A Ball Hut trip meant that Fyfe had to prepare provisions and horses for a morning start. Tracks had to be kept open, Ball Hut well stocked, and all the gear maintained in good condition — quite apart from helping tourists to plan their trips and ensuring their safety and comfort while they were away from the Hermitage, sometimes in tricky, even dangerous, conditions.

Successful guides have to be not only fit, expert and resourceful at all times, but also socially at ease, able to converse amiably with strangers, helping the tourists to enjoy themselves and perhaps interest them in climbing. Peter Graham summed up Tom Fyfe's personality as follows: '[He] had a genial disposition and a dry humour. In lighter moments he loved to tease, and with a mischievous twinkle in his eye he would give an amused chuckle, when he could raise a bite. He was reserved about his climbs, and only spoke of them to those who were interested or asked for climbing advice, which he would give freely.'[4]

Among the first visitors over the Christmas period of 1896 were Malcolm Ross and his wife Forrest, accompanied by Dr Norman Cox with whom Tom Fyfe had climbed previously. They stayed for some weeks but guide duties to the glaciers kept Fyfe busy for some time before he and Malcolm could climb as a pair. Malcolm had been commissioned by the Premier, Richard Seddon, to prepare material for an illustrated guide book for the Alps, and he proposed to organise an expedition which would include Tom Fyfe, and which would be paid for by the government. Ross had letters from Seddon to various people which confirmed the government's underwriting the costs of accommodation and pack horses. But the other Ross, Alexander, the manager of the Hermitage, refused to comply unless he had written instructions from departmental officers in Christchurch. The impasse was resolved by the coincidental arrival at the Hermitage of a departmental officer whose authorisation was accepted.

Fyfe and Ross then set out on the first of a series of climbs in which they became as effective a pair as Fyfe and Graham had been. But this relationship was a different one, because although Fyfe and Ross were friends, Ross had engaged Fyfe as a guide. They planned to go up onto the Main Divide in preparation for finding a new pass to the West Coast. Their objective was Mt Haidinger (10,059 ft) which rises 6,000 feet from the western side of the Tasman Glacier presenting a worthy challenge to climbers. Most climbers today approach it either from the Grand Plateau at 8,000 feet or from the névé of the Fox Glacier, using as a base Pioneer Hut, also at 8,000 feet. In 1897 there was only Ball Hut, and climbs were made either from high bivouacs or from the valley floor. Mt Haidinger's South Peak had been climbed by Zurbriggen, Fitzgerald and Jack Clark in 1895 from the camp on

J.J. Kinsey intro-
duces Malcolm
Ross, right, to
Signor Veglio
Borsolino near the
Tasman Glacier in
1896. The social
rules and the
clothing conven-
tions of the times
are clearly evident.
Source: W.A. Kennedy
Collection, Canterbury
Museum

the Haast Ridge. (Fitzgerald did not appreciate the skill of Clark,
Fyfe's protégé, and deleted him from the published photograph
of this success (see p 148) and in the text he slighted Clark's
contribution to the climb.) Fyfe and Ross planned to ascend from
a completely different direction, leaving from De la Beche bivouac to climb in one day the 6,000 feet to Haidinger's North
Peak.

From the De la Beche corner Haidinger rises abruptly — two
mixed snow and rock ridges flanked by the Kaufmann and
Forrest-Ross glaciers, culminating in a steep rock ridge that
leads to the large chisel-shaped rock summit that sits astride the
Main Divide. This route is primarily a rock climb interspersed
with some steep snow and ice and thus offered climbers without
crampons the prospect of a quick ascent with little need for step

cutting in ice. It was the choice of such routes that was the key to many of Fyfe's successes. Although it had not been climbed from this direction, the approach was not unknown to Fyfe because it ran parallel to the route that he, Kronecker and Clark had used on their attempt on Glacier Peak in the 1893-94 season. This climb was to be the first of a series that Fyfe and Ross did together, climbs that were characterised by the speed and stamina of the two men.

Plans for an early departure came to nought, and they did not leave the bivouac until 5.15 am. Fyfe, the fitter of the two because of his guiding, led easily and quickly up the rock ridge to the snow line, Ross following closely. There they had a brief stop for a second breakfast, a look at the sunrise, a lighting up of their pipes and a well-earned rest. Their view from that alpine balcony at that time of day was awe inspiring — massive drops on either side of the ridge into the glaciers, and the full extent of the Malte Brun Range with its high rock summits bathed in morning sunlight. The way ahead was also impressive, and their anticipation of the climb was doubtless heightened by the unknown.

On this photograph Fyfe marked the route he and Malcolm Ross used to ascend the North Peak of Mt Haidinger in 1897.
Source: J.J. Kinsey Collection, Canterbury Museum

The ridge on their right towards the summit looked open to

rockfall and quite unsafe. Fyfe quickly discounted it as a route. Ross agreed, later writing: 'The whole face of the rocky buttress was raked with the fire of falling stones, more deadly than the most destructive artillery. The chances were a thousand to one that, had we chosen that route, we should have met with swift and certain death.'[5] The route they chose bore away to the left, and after a quick dash across a comparatively low plateau overhung with the dangerous ice cliffs of the Kaufmann Glacier, they gained some firm rock climbing. Before negotiating a very steep narrow ridge, they agreed that if either of them fell the other would dive over the other side of the ridge — the only hope, they believed, of stopping a fall. Then came a section that Fyfe declared was 'sharp enough to cut bread with'.[6] Above it rose the massive rock face which forms the most prominent feature of the Haidinger's summit. Now the really difficult climbing began. They gradually ascended the steep face that was seamed with ice, cutting steps occasionally and finally gaining the last section.

Time was passing quickly and haste became necessary if they were to reach the top. The crux of the climb now presented itself.

Another view of Mt Haidinger, left, with Mt Douglas, to the right. A contoured series of icefalls and steep rock ridges, these slopes have rarely been climbed since Fyfe and Ross's success in 1897. They climbed to the base of the buttress and across to the icefield on the right before ascending to the summit.
Photo: Colin Monteath, Hedgehog House

155

Ross wrote: 'We made fair progress for a while, but at length we were brought to a standstill by a smooth sloping slab of rock that offered neither hand nor foothold. We could have cut up the shady side of the ridge and avoided this obstacle, but there was now no time for step cutting. It was the rocks or nothing.'[7] Once again Fyfe changed from nailed boots to rubber-soled shoes. Ross took a belay and gave him a leg up. The rope went out slowly and then stopped. Ross asked nervously if Fyfe had a good position to hold a fall. Fyfe replied laconically, 'No, not at all good.' Ross then proceeded to climb up with some caution. When further difficulties confronted them Fyfe led off again, this time leaving his ice axe behind so that he could climb more freely. In this way the last steep pitch was overcome and they stood on the crest of the Main Divide.

They were on an unclimbed summit — the North Peak of Mt Haidinger. Around them lay a dazzling array of peaks. Some distance along the ridge the South Peak of Haidinger rose some twenty-seven feet higher. They also had marvellous views across the Fox and Franz Josef Glaciers and huge areas of unclimbed terrain.

They could have only a brief spell at the summit, because they had a difficult descent and had to be off the mountain by nightfall. They were on steep rock and had to move cautiously. However, Fyfe's decision to leave his ice axe below meant that he had both his hands free to search for the holds. Of Fyfe's progress down, Ross wrote: 'With my face turned to the wall I could look between my legs and see Fyfe immediately below, cautiously feeling his way down … We wasted no time, but climbed steadily without a halt for that grim precipice still lay below.'[8] Their situation was very dangerous, and Fyfe was hit on the leg by loose rotten rock, suffering a bad gash, and Ross was stunned when he was struck on the head.

They had no option but to keep going, however, and after successfully negotiating the steepest sections they finally made easier ground to the point where they could begin glissading down snow slopes. Just as evening fell they reached the De la Beche bivouac. Here they were greeted by Ross's wife, Forrest, and Hodgkins who feasted them royally with such provisions as they had at their disposal — porridge, stewed peaches and mulligatawny soup — each course made in succession in the same billy much as climbers still do today.

Following the success on Mt Haidinger, Fyfe and Ross turned their attention to the Minarets, the then unclimbed 10,000 foot peaks which lie north of Mt De la Beche. Named for their shape, they offered the prospect of an attractive climb from the bivouac rock. Because he had already climbed Mt De la Beche some three years earlier with George Graham, Fyfe considered that route finding should not be a problem.

By now Ross was fitter, and making a 3.15 am departure, they climbed the Rudolf Glacier and arrived at the top of Mt De la Beche at 7.55 am. Even by today's standards that was fast climbing, especially without crampons. After a brief rest they made the sharp descent to the broad plateau separating the Minarets from Mt De la Beche in safety. It began with some careful rock climbing down to the plateau and then some intricate downhill cutting of steps in the ice. Within a short time they were on top of the Minarets, gazing around them and taking photographs. To the north, rising almost vertically out of the Spencer and Whymper Glaciers, the huge flanks of Elie de Beaumont dominated the view. Another first ascent accomplished, they quickly descended to the bivouac. They were back there by the middle of the afternoon, having run down the last mile of ice on the glaciers. With plenty of time available, they pressed on further, having decided to exchange the dubious comforts of the bivouac for a bunk at Ball Hut.

Fyfe's and Ross's next journey, over Lendenfeld Saddle and down the Whataroa River to the West Coast, contained all the varied demands of New Zealand climbing last century. Climbers of those days were necessarily like explorers who sometimes became alpinists; they were more than mountaineers whose skills were focused on snow, ice and rock on precipitous slopes. Besides scaling virgin peaks they found routes on uncharted glaciers, discovered new passes, pushed through dense forest and crossed raging torrents. There were no alternatives or aids to

The author and party are in the foreground of this 1978 view of the classical symmetry of the Minarets, first climbed by Fyfe and Ross in 1897.
Photo: David Hughes.

the laborious exploration these two men were about to undertake with their primitive equipment. To this day their journey has not been repeated.

At just under 8,000 feet in height, Lendenfeld Saddle lies where the mighty Tasman Glacier begins. On that side it is a broad undulating expanse of névé snow towards the north-west, but towards the West Coast the terrain drops away sharply to the Whymper Glacier — so sharply that from the Hochstetter Dome or from Elie de Beaumont much of its catchment area is hidden from view. An amphitheatre of rock and ice falls for thousands of feet at an appalling angle. There were distinct possibilities that they might get themselves bluffed at any time and be forced to return up difficult terrain to the saddle. With only ice axes and a hempen rope as their climbing equipment, they set out to make a new crossing to the West Coast.

The two men had similar personal ambitions to explore the area and find new routes, and they each had their own career motives — Ross to write for a government-sponsored publication, and

Fyfe to find a suitable tourist route to the West Coast which would extend up the Tasman Glacier from Ball Hut and from Brodrick Hut then under construction. Fyfe wrote to his wife that there was absolutely no danger in the undertaking — an assurance that was quite unjustified by the events. The pair were farewelled by their friends at the Hermitage on 18 February 1897. They made Ball Hut that day, and next day pushed on to De la Beche bivouac laden with heavy packs where, to conserve their own rations for what lay ahead, they ate some three-week-old bread they found there.

Moving across the glacier to the Malte Brun bivouac, they slept in the very spot in the tussock where Fyfe and Kronecker had camped four years earlier. They even found some items that Kronecker had mislaid there — a lantern, a pen knife and a leather field-glass case. At 1 am Fyfe and Ross woke, and by dawn they were onto Lendenfeld Saddle where they surveyed the nearby peaks bathed in the red rays of a summer sunrise. Elie de Beaumont's rounded snow-covered summit showed up well, but below them on the other side the prospect looked ominous. At the sight of the huge ice and rock chasm dropping to the Whymper Glacier, Fyfe begged Ross, 'Don't say a blessed word till we've had a smoke, and then we'll look around.'[9] Ross wrote: 'I acquiesced, and we sat down on the rocks, munched a few figs and some chocolate, and then had a smoke and the look around. We were not enamoured of the prospect. The panorama certainly was magnificent, especially towards the north-east; but the getting down, that was the trouble.'[10]

They tried to gauge the height. Fyfe estimated that it was about four thousand feet down to the Whymper Glacier, and between them and the Whymper lay steep ice and unstable rock. With typical optimism, he thought that if they could get into an avalanche gully which they could see away to the west and far below, then it might provide access to the upper reaches of the glacier.

After the usual checks of gear and clothing, they commenced the descent with a short climb down steep rotten rock where they had to use a short rope and to take extreme care not to fall.

Continuing onto a small avalanche-prone snow slope, they then headed down towards the avalanche path they were aiming for. The way was barred, however, by a large icefall which forced them to climb through some dangerous seracs. Eventually they gained a steep rock ridge down which lay the only route. But it was nearly vertical, the type of obstacle that climbers today overcome with an abseil.

Ross wrote, 'We were face to face with a precipice down which it was impossible for man to climb. We thought we should give it up as hopeless, but we pondered the situation, and then began to scan the ridge immediately behind on our left. Here an almost vertical slab of wet rock, between thirty and forty feet, led into a narrow gulch or chimney, down which a waterfall was pouring. There were no hand-holds to speak of — only one or two cracks in the rock — but I thought I could get down.'[11] They had to decide whether to turn back or try to climb down this rock, because once they were over it, they would be committed to continue.

They decided to go ahead, and now the full repertoire of Fyfe's

Fyfe packs his swag after sleeping in the open on the Malte Brun Range before the Malte Brun Hut was built in 1898. Brushwood has been collected to form a mattress, and blankets are drying on the warm rocks.

Photo: Kinsey Collection, Canterbury Museum

skills came into play. Using a rope that had been cut by a rock earlier in the day and was now held together with a fisherman's bend, first Ross made the descent and then was quickly joined by Fyfe. When they had successfully negotiated this section, Fyfe pointed out the need for speed as the place they were in was menaced by more falling seracs. Now into the icefall, they navigated across it towards the avalanche gully they had picked as the likeliest route onto the Whymper Glacier which was still far below them. Because of their early start and the speed with which they had moved, the sun's warmth had not yet taken effect and the avalanche-prone slopes far above them remained frozen. Nothing fell on them as they took turns to execute belayed glissades down the gully, eyes to the front on the lookout for crevasses, but ears cocked for the first sound of debris falling behind them.

At the foot of the gully where the fallen ice fans out in a semi-circle they knew they were reasonably safe. Now they walked for the first time on the upper névé of the Whymper Glacier. As

Panorama of Lendenfeld Saddle from the Whymper Glacier side, with Elie de Beaumont, right, Mt Cook, centre, and Hochstetter Dome, left. Fyfe and Ross descended to the Whymper from the saddle through the icefalls.
Photo: Gavin Wills

161

climbers often do when they are out of danger, having shared tense moments and trusted their luck and skill to the limit, they stopped and shook hands, pleased no doubt to be still alive. They had been descending for nine hours non-stop and they sat down and ate their lunch on the glacier.

By late afternoon they had made some progress down the upper glacier, and so with the weather still holding fine they made camp at 6 pm. 'We ate a frugal meal of tinned meat, bread and tea, made a mattress of damp green branches and ferns cut with our pocket-knives, crept into our sleeping bags, lit our pipes, talked over the events of the day and the prospects of the morrow and then tried to sleep.'[12] Now the injury Fyfe had received on Mt Haidinger began to cause trouble — not surprising considering the sixteen-hour-day over extremely rough terrain.

They now faced the special problems of journeying in the wilds of the West Coast. In their path lay formidable obstacles: enormous boulders, the Whataroa River, and steep gorges carved into the rock. In its upper reaches the Whataroa is one of Westland's most difficult rivers. It drains an immense catchment area extending from the Garden of Eden Ice Plateau and circling around to the upper regions of the Main Divide beyond the Godley Glacier. Encompassing a full mountain range, the Butler, which lies wholly in Westland, it collects all the melt water from the Whymper Glacier and the flanks of Elie de Beaumont and the Maximilian Range. There was no map of the area, and Fyfe and Ross had no idea of the number of glaciers that fed into the river.

The dawn start that followed their night's sleep found Fyfe limping badly, and while clambering over and through the large boulders of the riverbed his leg was struck twice, injuring it further. They changed to bush crashing as the best means of progress, and soon had the good fortune to find a hot spring, one of a number of such delights on that side of the Main Divide. It is not difficult to imagine their satisfaction or the relief to their aching limbs. Refreshed, they now made good progress, keeping mainly to the bush on the hillside until that evening when they reached a deep gorge. With his leg still troubling him, Fyfe was reluctant to try to negotiate it, and so they pitched camp for their second night in Westland.

Fortunately the weather held. If it had not they might have been trapped by the river's rising to a level that would make it impossible to cross. But Fyfe's injured leg had now swollen to an abnormal size, causing great pain and fever, and they had to stay where they were for the whole day. They were now at risk of survival — one injured in a party of two, far from help, and their food running low. With only a small amount of bread left to sustain them, they settled into a convenient sandbank, having scooped out hollows for their hips. Not surprisingly, with Fyfe moaning in agony, little sleep was had, and with a major river to cross in the morning their prospects looked grim.

But he was able to walk next morning, so they rose from their uncomfortable bivouac at 5 am to tackle the river when it was at its shallowest. The first stream presented no difficulties but the second was swifter and deeper. Even though he was injured, Fyfe went first, encumbered with swag, rope and ice axe. Almost immediately he was out of his depth. But he was a strong swimmer and he somehow managed to get himself across to a point where he was able to stand. The current knocked him over again before he finally reached the bank. It had been a close call, and all he could do was laugh at the good fortune which had again got him through. He then tried to help Ross, who had been watching nervously, by throwing the rope across to him, but it was not long enough. Ross then moved to a different point and managed to make his own crossing and join Fyfe triumphantly on the other bank.

The worst of the journey was now over and they soon came across some fresh footprints which they believed were those of a gold-miner working nearby. After four or five hours of easier walking, to their surprise they came across a young boy who turned out to be the son of Alex Gunn of the Whataroa Ferry. Lunchtime saw them at the one house which constituted the settlement then known as Rohutu. They had completed the first and only crossing of Lendenfeld Saddle from the Tasman Glacier to the West Coast.

163

Two 1930s climbers struggle against the deep and swift current of the Whataroa River, just as Fyfe and Ross had done in 1897.

Photo: D.V. Apperley, W.A. Kennedy Collection, Canterbury Museum

Fyfe's leg was now so inflamed that he travelled to Hokitika where Dr Teichelmann opened it up and took out two or three pieces of bone — making nonsense of Tom's assurance to Annie about there being no danger. Malcolm Ross decided to return to the Hermitage over the Fitzgerald Pass; in doing so he became one of the first to make the crossing from west to east in that region and the first person to cross it solo. When Fyfe was able to travel he returned to Timaru, but the injured leg later became gangrenous. His son Malcolm Fyfe says that his father's leg was saved only by the hot poultices made by Tom's Scottish grandmother, who for many days kept applying them to the affected limb.

A return to the Hermitage now was out of the question, and the climbing season was virtually over anyway. It was some years before Fyfe could use the leg in sustained walking, but in the meantime he began work at Albury. When the injury improved sufficiently to enable him to move more freely he was again employed by the Department of Lands and Survey. In 1898 he was stationed at Hanmer near the hot springs resort, close to the alpine scenery he loved so much.

The Department offered the position of guide at Mt Cook to Jack Clark, who now had excellent credentials. Clark said he would accept only if Fyfe was not available. Tom Fyfe's misfortune became Jack Clark's good luck and they remained close friends.

1. Department of Lands and Survey, S3041, Christchurch: National Archives, 30 November 1896.
2. *AJHR*, Annual Report. Department of Lands and Survey. C1. 1897.
3. Department of Lands and Survey, S3041.
4. P. Graham, "Tom Fyfe: In Memoriam," *NZAJ* Vol. 15, (June 1953): 287.
5. Ross, *A Climber in New Zealand*, p.147.
6. Ibid., p.148.
7. Ibid., p.149.
8. *New Zealand Times*, 5 June 1897.
9   Ibid.
10. Ibid.
11. Ibid.
12. Ross, p. 298.

12

FIRST TRAVERSE OF MT COOK

The injury to Fyfe's leg in February 1897 was enough to keep him from serious climbing for some years. In 1902 he was working for the Public Works Department in Wellington, but his mountaineering skills had not been forgotten by the Tourist Department, and when they wanted his services in 1905 he was keen to help them. He was then married with three children, but still only thirty-five, and the opportunity of climbing again at a high level was too attractive to turn down.

The opening came when the superintendent of the department, T.E. Donne, attended a lecture in London presented by the climber and explorer, Samuel Turner, to the Geographical Society. Donne was anxious to make New Zealand's tourist attractions better known and he proposed to Turner that he attempt the first traverse of Mt Cook. In return for the government's meeting his expenses, Turner would write a series of articles for newspapers, thus advertising New Zealand's alpine attractions. With the increased popularity of the Hermitage, it was evident to Donne that Jack Clark would be fully employed with the tourists and climbs for the season, and that Fyfe would have more time to devote to Turner's expedition. Turner would be free to climb where he wished and Fyfe would assess how well his client adjusted to New Zealand conditions. At Fyfe's insistence, his old climbing partner, Malcolm Ross, was added to the party, thus in some measure returning favours that Ross had arranged for him.

On his arrival at Mt Cook near the height of the climbing season late in December 1905, Turner was keen to climb a virgin peak, and Elie de Beaumont became his objective. At 10,200 feet it stands as a magnificent corner-post, and being above the Spencer, Whymper and Tasman Glaciers it radiates steep rock ridges and ice faces down into the depths of many valleys. Viewed to advantage from Franz Josef, it fills the head of the Callery valley

The first women to cross Copland Pass, 1903: left to right are: Miss Barnicoat, J. Smith, Jack Clark, Miss Perkins (front), Mrs Thomson, E. Fluckiger (Swiss guide).
Photo: W.A. Kennedy Collection, Canterbury Museum

as an outstanding mountain — more than merely another peak on the alpine chain as are some of its neighbouring summits.

It had not been climbed because access to it was difficult, the approach to the mountain from the Tasman Glacier often cut off by large crevasses in the Anna Glacier. Turner, Fyfe and Ross set out for Elie de Beaumont shortly after arriving at Mt Cook, but their first attempt was thwarted by bad weather. There was a good deal of fresh deep snow for that time of the year, and the week before, a party arriving at Malte Brun Hut had had to dig down through the snow to get to the door. Fyfe and his party returned to Ball Hut and by Christmas the weather cleared sufficiently for them to start for a preparatory climb on the Liebig Range.

The Nuns Veil at almost 9,000 feet provides one of the most spectacular viewpoints in the Mt Cook area, and, still unclimbed at that time, it was thought a worthy objective. It has a large rock buttress facing west, and beyond this towards the south-east there comes down from the summit in a series of steps toward the valley floor the Nuns Veil Glacier, an uninterrupted flow of

May Kinsey, daughter of J.J. Kinsey, washing outside Ball Hut, 1895. In those days the hut gave only rudimentary shelter, the floor consisting of flat rocks placed on the ground by successive groups, and all cooking and washing was done outside.

Photo: Kinsey Collection, Canterbury Museum

white. Directly to the north lie several other fine rock peaks with ecclesiastical names — Mt Biretta, Monastery Peak, The Abbot and The Abbess.

On approaching their objective, the party found that what had seemed an easy rock ridge became less so. Fyfe, enjoying the challenge, was keen to continue leading along this ridge but Turner suggested proceeding down a snow couloir — a decision which seems to have cost them the first ascent as they found they were now unable to get to their peak. Because Mt Biretta was close at hand they tackled that instead — the first ascent of that mountain. After a careful descent they returned to their camp and on 27 December they departed again for Malte Brun Hut and Elie de Beaumont.

Next morning the prospects for a fine day were not good, but Turner decided that they should try for Elie de Beaumont again via the Anna Glacier. After passing the foot of Mt Walter, which is prone to rockfall, they were threading their way up through the large snow fields and seracs when the weather deteriorated.

168

Peter Graham, who was guiding a party on Hochstetter Dome that same day and aware of Turner's party, later wrote: 'While we were putting on the rope for the final approach to the peak we were enveloped in a thick cloud and snow began to fall. We watched the other party's ascent until they, too, disappeared in a cloud blanket ... there was no visibility, it had become very cold, and under these circumstances it was unwise to proceed. So we turned back, retreating to the hut. It was not until two hours later that we saw Mr Turner's party returning. We thought they might have made the summit but were certain they would have seen nothing.'[1]

Carrying a full swag, and bearded after a week's climbing on the Liebig Range, Fyfe crosses the Murchison River in 1905.
Photo: Malcolm Ross.

In fact they had not reached the summit, although they were quite near it. The cold had become intense and with a very strong wind on the upper slopes they had held onto their positions only with great difficulty. Fyfe and Ross had been keen to beat a retreat earlier because of the conditions, but at Turner's request had kept on until it became plain to all that they would not reach the summit that day. Peter Graham commented sardonically that 'Mr Turner, being a very determined man, had wished to show his prowess by continuing'.[2]

Fyfe, Turner and Ross made two further attempts on the peak but each time the weather was against them. Elie de Beaumont's majestic summit icecap remained unconquered until Peter Graham and Hendrik Sillem, a Dutch climber, made the first ascent in February 1906, having much more favourable conditions than earlier in the season. On the summit they found that, like a planet with its attendant moons, it had an outlying peak that was also over 10,000 feet high.

The attempts on Elie de Beaumont and the Nuns Veil were part of a programme for Turner that Fyfe hoped would progressively acquaint him with the conditions in the New Zealand mountains. Those climbs had also helped Fyfe to regain his fitness and at the same time enabled him to assess Turner's capabilities. Peter Graham, who by then had had two seasons' guiding at Mt Cook, thought that Turner was bombastic, but there is no reason to believe that Fyfe and Turner did not get on with one another. Fyfe encouraged Turner's interest in the New Zealand mountains during this first visit, and Turner went on to achieve many notable climbs, including the first ascent of Mt Tutoko with Peter Graham as his guide.

The preparation that Fyfe, Turner and Ross had undertaken for the attempt to traverse Mt Cook had been less than ideal, but Fyfe must have been satisfied with Turner's mountaineering skills. He was also confident of Ross's ability and endurance notwithstanding his age — then forty-five — but Ross had sprained his ankle. Jack Clark had been asked by the superintendent of the Tourist Department to attach Peter Graham to Turner's party to give him more experience, and with Ross a

A formidable climbing trio — left to right, Tom Fyfe, Malcolm Ross and the young Peter Graham — before their 1906 traverse of the High Peak of Mt Cook, accompanied by Samuel Turner.
Source: Malcolm Ross

doubtful starter Graham became second guide to Fyfe. When Ross's ankle improved so that he could rejoin the party, it became a very strong climbing team with a balance of experience and youth.

The proposed route was up the long Zurbriggen Ridge, which comprised mixed snow and ice climbing and involved considerable exposure down onto Mt Cook's East Face. The plan was to climb this ridge to the summit, then descend via the steep rock of the North Ridge, and thence down the icy 2,000 foot couloir to the Hooker Glacier. Tom Fyfe's intimate knowledge of the North Ridge from the first ascent of Mt Cook would be invaluable, as would Peter Graham's of Zurbriggen Ridge when he had climbed Mt Cook the season before in Jack Clark's party. This traverse demands a very high standard of climbing skill on both ice and rock and it has seldom been repeated.

In 1905 not one major peak in the Mt Cook region had been traversed. A complete traverse — up one side of a mountain and down the other, instead of descending by the way of the ascent — requires great skill and confidence. The special hazards of traversing are on the descent. Climbers have not only to find a route down with no upwards steps to guide them as would usually be the case, but on the descent itself they have to cut steps in ice below them. This is much more difficult and dangerous than cutting steps while moving upwards.

It is clear from the three separate accounts written by Samuel Turner, Malcolm Ross and Peter Graham, that Tom Fyfe was determined to complete the climb as planned and thus add to his first ascent the first traverse of the peak. It is also evident that in doing so he pushed himself and his party near to the limit of what mountaineers were capable of at the time with the equipment they had. Although the three accounts do not disagree on essential facts, each author wrote, of course, from his own point of view, noting strengths and weaknesses of the other members of the party.

The climb began on 8 January 1906 with an ascent to the bivouac site on the Haast Ridge. During the next day the weather improved and conditions on Mt Cook became more suitable. They busied themselves in preparation for the day ahead. Fyfe, who was well able to prepare a hearty meal in camps if sufficient food was available, fed the party and melted snow to obtain drinking water for the climb ahead. He was first to rise, stirring the group into departing well before midnight on 9 January. Cameras, extra clothing and sufficient food were chosen with a view to lightness, but their packs still weighed between fifteen and twenty pounds. They planned to take the first photographs from the summit of Mt Cook, because it seemed that those taken by Zurbriggen in 1895 were from below the peak.

The previous afternoon Fyfe and Graham had kicked steps over Glacier Dome and down towards the Grand Plateau. Now the long slope of Zurbriggen Ridge came into sight quickly, and in bright moonlight Fyfe quickly led the party across this expanse of snow and ice. When they reached the base of the ridge Peter Graham explored a way across the large bergschrund. Above this obstacle the angle of the ridge steepened and Tom Fyfe took the lead again. They had two ropes with them, but they climbed on one and in soft snow made good progress. Graham recalled: 'We could kick steps in places and with some cutting here and there we edged towards the rock ridge. But we proceeded on up on the snow as the rocks were so ice-covered. The snow was deep in places. After we had gone about 1000 feet, Fyfe unfortunately bumped his shin badly against a hidden rock and opened up an old wound which he had suffered some years before on the crossing of the Lendenfeld with Mr Ross. It was swollen and painful.'[3]

The snow and ice slope up which they were climbing is approximately 3,000 feet long and it continues until it meets the rocks of the ridge. Graham now took over the lead to relieve Fyfe. The angle of the slope increased and as the exposure became more severe great care was needed with rope management, all members having to keep alert lest a fall or slip by one of them should need to be halted quickly. With Graham leading strongly, they climbed off the slope and onto the ridge at 6.30 am. They quickly ate a second breakfast, and although appreciating the spectacular view resplendent in the dawn, they soon turned upwards again and pushed on to the summit. Graham led on up the summit rocks which were iced, and Fyfe, having recovered somewhat from the injury to his leg, then began to cut steps up the ice ridge toward the final schrund. At this point he again changed the order of the rope and let Graham lead to the summit, which they reached at one o'clock, almost fourteen hours after leaving their camp site. From his experience more than eleven years earlier, Fyfe calculated that they had sufficient time to descend the North Ridge if it was in good climbing order and not covered in ice, and that they could reach the Hooker Glacier before nightfall.

But first, after the long sustained climbing, the summit offered a chance to take in the stupendous view and to rest aching muscles and taut nerves. The first photographs from the top of Mt Cook were duly taken and the smokers in the party lit up, but after only twenty-five minutes' rest the descent began. Fyfe had planned to take the pulses of the party for scientific record but

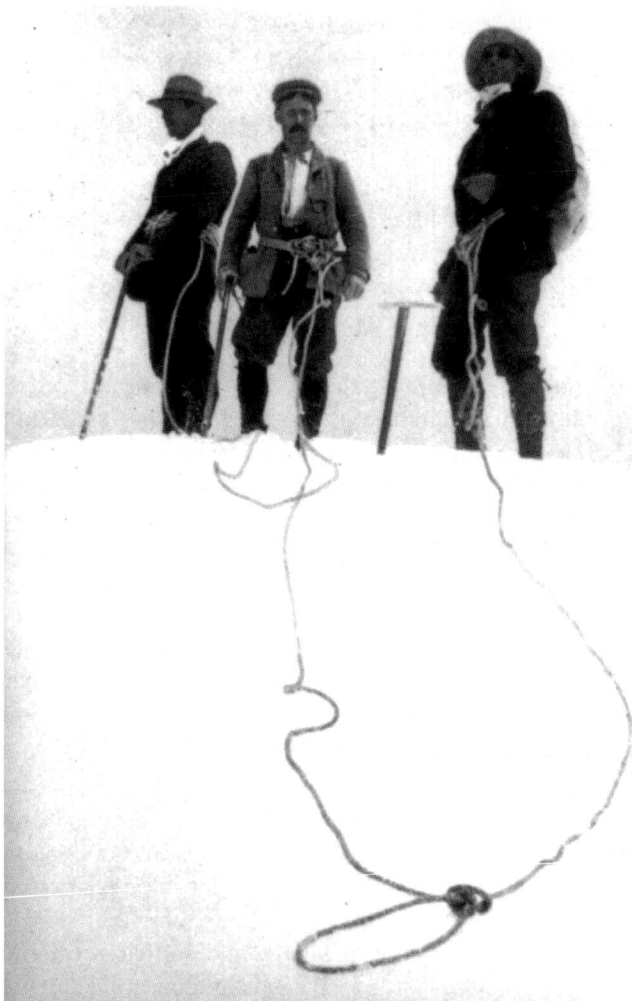

Peter Graham, left, Samuel Turner, centre, and Tom Fyfe on the High Peak of Mt Cook during the 1906 traverse. In the foreground lies Malcolm Ross's climbing rope which he has undone in order to secure this photograph.
Photo: Malcolm Ross

did not do so — preferring, perhaps to enjoy the view.. Doubtless
he would have recalled his first visit to this spot with Jack Clark
and George Graham. Now he faced the task of climbing down by
the same route they had taken in 1894.

As on the ascent, the two guides now shared the responsibility
for a safe descent, Peter Graham moving down the icecap first
with Tom Fyfe ever watchful as the anchor man at the rear. With
his muscular build and strong arms Fyfe was well able to hold a
man, yet the equipment of the day was such that only the
smallest slip could be checked with safety. To a large extent the
only real protection against a fatal fall was the skill and balance
of the climbers. Fortunately this party was exceptionally skilled,
and even when they found that the ridge was smothered in ice
they did not give serious thought to returning by the line of
ascent. They could make only slow progress on the steep rock,
however, despite Fyfe's instructions, of which Ross wrote: 'Fyfe
repeatedly urged him [Turner] to hurry and trust for safety to the
rope. I came next, and Turner was between me and Graham,
who, under general direction from Fyfe, led down.'[4]

Even now the climb of this ridge is graded very highly in level of
difficulty, and to descend when it is iced is a hazardous undertaking. The party had to take extreme care if they were to get
down safely; each climber had to have complete trust in the
abilities of the others as well as his own. Ross described the
problems in detail: 'After descending a few hundred feet, we
soon found that, owing to the ice-glazing and the new snow, it
was impossible to keep to the crest of the ridge and the descent
became largely a series of traverses across difficult and, at time,
precipitous faces of rock, most on the eastern side of the arête.
On the crest the climbing was even more difficult, and there was
a bitter wind blowing so we avoided that side as much as
possible. In one place we had to climb back from the eastern face
through a gap of overhanging rock and great icicles. Peter
smashed the greater part of the icicles with the handle of his ice-
axe, and the broken pieces went swishing down the precipice
towards the Hooker.'[5]

Progress was now painstakingly slow. Fyfe kept urging Graham on in the quest for a route until two steep rock steps were met. Here the rope had to be taken off, and each member lowered over. This manoeuvre was accomplished, but not without some dramatic moments — yawning depths gaped thousands of feet below climbers twirling on the end of the rope, scratching for footholds. Turner insisted that he would be able to climb down, but he could not and had to be lowered like the others. Graham records that Fyfe grinned broadly as he let Turner down the rope with a series of jerks. As the last climber, Fyfe could not be lowered and had to resort to hitching the rope over the precarious rock and then sliding down.

It was 6.45 pm before they reached Green Saddle situated above the couloir that leads to the Hooker. Although they were not completely off the mountain by nightfall, there was the prospect of a descent before long, provided that the snow was in good order. But Mt Cook did not relent easily, and when the condition of the couloir was tested it was found to be ice. Fyfe, keen to make all haste, shouted to Graham to kick steps, but this was not possible and steps had to be cut. Their luck was holding with the weather, however, and with darkness falling, Graham began cutting steps down the couloir. In an outstanding performance with the ice-axe, he did most of the cutting for five cold hours, relieved at times by Fyfe. To free Graham for this, Fyfe hoisted Graham's pack on top of his own, giving him perhaps forty pounds to carry and keep balanced as he sought the steps in the darkness. The only mishap was that Turner was hit by a falling rock, but he was not badly hurt. Shortly after midnight they gained the bergschrund at the top of the Hooker Glacier that had caused Fyfe so much concern on the first ascent. They soon passed it, and thus could say that they were off the mountain, and that the first traverse of Mt Cook's highest peak had been completed.

Their second dawn found them slowly threading their way down the glacier towards the Hermitage, having taken thirty-six hours, incorporating a day and two nights. They were welcomed back by the managers, the MacDonald family, and the other guides. Fyfe and Graham sat down to an enormous breakfast, and later they celebrated their success over a bottle of wine with

Tom Fyfe, aged thirty-six, outside the Hermitage before the 1906 traverse.
Source: Peter Graham, *Mountain Guide*

Malcolm Ross. Fyfe thanked Peter Graham for his support and assistance, and in turn Graham later wrote that what pleased him most was Fyfe's congratulations and his warm appreciation of his help.

As had happened after the first ascent of Mt Cook, whatever co-operation and companionship there had been on the traverse disappeared when two of the party fell out over the reporting of this notable achievement. On the way down the valley Ross and

Turner had discussed this matter. Turner feared that Ross, with his journalistic skills and contacts, might report on the climb first and thus affect Turner's arrangements with the government. Ross assured Turner that he would not do that, but when Turner's press release about the climb showed only his own name, Ross was so furious that in his report, published in the *Lyttelton Times,* he described Turner as a travelling tourist from London. The rancour between the two showed in their later writings, and, as Wilson put it, 'Ross is a conspicuous omission from Turner's generous thanks to his companions in the foreword of his *Conquest of the New Zealand Alps*'.[5]

Shortly after their return, plans were discussed for an attempt on Mt Sefton (10,359 ft) which stands sentinel high above the Hermitage — a massive entanglement of ice and rock rising steeply against the western sky. It had been climbed only once before, in 1895 by Zurbriggen and Fitzgerald, and as its approach offered such challenging climbing it was an attractive proposition that would match the skills of Fyfe and Graham. Unfortunately the rock ridge that leads to the summit was seen to be heavily covered in snow and in that condition an ascent would have been a most difficult task. Their plans for that climb were therefore abandoned.

1. P. Graham, *Mountain Guide: an autobiography,* (Wellington: Reed, 1965), p.108.
2. Ibid., p.109.
3. Ibid., p.111.
4. Ross, *A Climber in New Zealand,* p.298.
5. J. Wilson, *Aorangi,* (Christchurch: Whitcombe & Tombs, 1968), p.119.

13

LAST CLIMBS

Between 1897 and 1905 Tom and Annie Fyfe had been focused more on their family than on Tom's climbing. Their eldest daughter, Lila Aorangi, was born in 1898; then came Kenneth in 1903, another daughter, Clyde, in 1905, and then Malcolm in 1907. The children's names had close associations with their father's mountaineering exploits: Aorangi is an alternative name for Mt Cook, Kenneth and Malcolm were the Christian names of the Ross brothers and Clyde refers to a major tributary of the Rangitata River.

They lived in Wellington from 1902 until 1905 when Tom took leave to lead Turner on the first traverse of Mt Cook. He then returned to work in Wellington, but the attraction of again living in South Canterbury might have been rekindled by that great climb. Their decision to move back to Timaru might also have been partly due, however, to a work accident. On 27 March 1906 Fyfe was badly injured when a heavy block fell on his arm while he was repairing lifts in the General Post Office. Unable to resume his job until 20 April,[1] he resigned ten days later, moved back to Timaru and took up residence in Wilson Street next door to his relatives.

There was no shortage of work, and being already well known in the area he quickly re-established himself, but with a family to support, his mountaineering trips now took place during annual holidays. It was an unsettled period in his life, however, as his work often took him away from home. Possibly torn between family responsibilities and the satisfactions of climbing, he is remembered as now being quietly spoken, very self-reliant, reading a great deal and seldom talking about himself.

However, in 1908 George Mannering, his old climbing companion, suggested to him that they explore the mountains between Lake Tekapo and the Hermitage, and Tom Fyfe accepted the

179

Malcolm Ross on
the Minarets,
January 1897.
Photo: Tom Fyfe

invitation. They hoped to find a route over the Liebig Range that
would be suitable for tourist walkers and would connect with
the system of huts on the Tasman Glacier and make a round trip
from Tekapo. The Tourist Department had been interested in the
scenic possibilities of such a trip. In 1906 Peter Graham and
George Rose, a publisher and photographer from Melbourne,
had explored a route over the Tasman Saddle and Murchison
Glacier into the Godley valley and down to Tekapo. The disadvantage was that it was a long trip and in parts difficult for the
uninitiated.

The first opportunity that suited both Fyfe and Mannering was in
the holiday period between 1908 and 1909. It started as a leisurely
excursion, for instead of taking the train and coach as in days gone
by, they left Timaru by motor car on Christmas Day and in the
afternoon did some trout fishing at Tekapo. Early on Boxing Day
John Rutherford of Mistake Station (now Godley Peaks) accompanied them in their journey up the Cass River. The following day
with a packhorse and a station hand to assist them, they began the
long approach walk through the barren landscape which led to
the upper hut some miles above the station.

Here the mountain views became spectacular, Mt Radove

R.L. Wigley brings
mail from Fairlie to
the Hermitage in
1907 in a De Dion
8 h.p. car. The
advent of cars cut
this trip from two
days to one.
Photo: Mt Cook and
Southern Lakes Tourist
Company.

(7,914ft) dominating the view to the east and Mt Hutton (9,297 ft) filling the head of the Faraday Glacier. Mt Radove was named after Nicolo (Big Mick) Radove who had purchased The Mistake in 1875 after selling Birch Hill. With its bulky appearance and a reputation as a tough nut to crack, the mountain was thought to mirror its namesake. It has been written of Radove that: 'Prosperous times induced him to spend money freely. Town visitors revelled in The Mistake parties that went on for a week, and when the beer ran out, Big Mick drove down to the Tekapo Hotel to bring back another hogshead full. If guests tired of drinking, they could enjoy cakes flavoured with whisky. Big Mick's marriage brought more order to The Mistake but it came too late to avoid financial collapse. After losing two children they walked out of the station penniless.'[2]

Big Mick Radove's Birch Hill sheep station in 1869. An Italian veteran of the Crimean War, Radove is likely to have named Mt Sebastopol. Von Haast, exploring in the area, is said to have been surprised to find he was not alone — Big Mick was mustering on the ramparts above him.

Source: T.D. Burnett Collection

Heavy grazing of the valley of the Cass by the first owner, Sibbald of Lilybank, and then by Radove had left the vegetation sparse, but Fyfe and Mannering saw abundant bird life — paradise duck, gulls, and sooty terns, pied stilt and dotterel.

181

However, even by then there were only a few kea left further up the valley, probably because of bounties of between 2s 6d and 10s per bird. Next morning, with the weather unsettled, they left the horses with Rutherford's man and told him to remain at the hut until 5pm before returning home in case they had to turn back. As they made their way toward the head of the valley a route came into view up the Faraday Glacier. It looked relatively easy and Fyfe decided it would be a 'cake walk' — somewhat to Mannering's surprise, who wrote that 'Fyfe exhibited a strong desire to climb some of the fine peaks that were arrayed before them', including one which Mannering, described as being shaped like 'a little Matterhorn'.[3] They bestowed names on two unnamed features: Ridge Glacier, and Mt Lucia (8,500 ft), prominent to the south.

They now made their way up the west branch of the Cass to the upper part of the Ridge Glacier and after negotiating some crevasses climbed onto the main ridge. To the north lay the vast grey moraine of the Murchison Glacier which had first been visited by Mannering and his friends some nineteen years previously. Across the valley Malte Brun stood resplendent, its icy steep east-facing slopes glittering white, blue and pink in the morning sun — the summit of which Fyfe had reached some fifteen years earlier. They noticed a gap in the rock ridge and named it Rutherford Pass. It seemed a possible route to the Murchison, and on the other side they travelled comfortably on easy rock ridges to within 300 feet of the glacier. But at that point their difficulties began. Mannering wrote: 'On either hand were very steep ravines caused by falls of rock carving away the sides of the spur we were on and sharpening it up as one might sharpen a scythe. In vain we let each other out the length of a 50 ft rope on either side, and on the ridge itself. The rocks were absolutely rotten, and there was no safe hold anywhere. Nothing short of 200 feet of rope, and the probable sacrifice of most of that would have got us down that place.'[4]

The weather then began to change from merely threatening to thickly falling snow. Bluffed, all they could do was retrace their steps up through the scrub and the snow that soon covered everything. Retreats are dispiriting, but the desire to get down drives aching bodies on, and eventually they found a spur that led to the valley floor. Lacking top fitness and with no streams in sight, they relieved their raging thirsts by drinking water out of lily leaves. They finally reached the Murchison at 1 pm.

Their original intention was to camp in the Murchison and try to find a new pass over the Malte Brun Range to link their route with Malte Brun Hut. The managers at the Hermitage had lent them a silk tent so that they could camp out, but with the weather so bad the greater comfort of Ball Hut beckoned, and so they pushed on. They reached it at 5 pm, having made good time down the Murchison River and across the Tasman Glacier. The total time taken from the Cass had been thirteen hours. The following day they walked out to the Hermitage, and when the weather cleared the day after, they walked from Mt Cook Station to Lake Tekapo, there regaining their car.

Mannering and Fyfe believed that this round trip from Lake Tekapo to the Hermitage via the Cass, Murchison and Tasman glaciers could be used by tourists, but even with intermediate huts the distances and the barren and desolate environment would probably have appealed to only the most energetic visitors. This apart, Fyfe was impressed with the quality of some of the climbing in the valley of the Cass and he decided to return with a companion. J. R. Simpson and Fyfe later made the first ascent of Mt Lucia which he had just named.

He then again turned his attention to Mt Cook, mainly because in the time he had been away an interesting new route had been climbed to its summit. Mountaineering in the region was entering a new phase as the foundations laid by the early climbers, the Hermitage Company and the government were beginning to bear fruit. Tom Fyfe and then Jack Clark had established the traditions of safe climbing, and from 1903 these were carried on by Peter Graham and his guides at the Hermitage, and by Alex Graham on the West Coast. Visitor numbers to the Hermitage were rising each year and plans were made for a bigger and better replacement hotel.

There was much more interest in climbing. Good walkers were

being taken on easy climbs and then graduating to harder ascents. Women were becoming more active and ambitious. Forrest Ross, wife of Malcolm, was an active climber and in 1892 had become the first woman member of the New Zealand Alpine Club. In 1903 Mrs J. Thomson, Miss Perkins and Miss Barnicoat were the first party of women to cross the Copland Pass and later tackled much more difficult climbs. An Australian woman, Freda Du Faur, climbed Mt Cook with Alex and Peter Graham in 1910, and in 1911, with Peter Graham and Darby Thomson, she traversed Mt Cook up the West Ridge and down the Linda Glacier. In less than four years she did twenty-three separate climbs in the region.

The new route on Mt Cook was called Earle's route as a result of a climb in March 1907 when Jack Clark and Peter and Alex Graham had guided L. Earle, an English climber, up a rock rib from the Hooker Glacier. Fyfe was keen to climb it, and in March 1911 it was agreed that he would guide J. R. Simpson on it, with Jack Clark as the third member of the party.

The weather continued a long, fine spell as it sometimes does late in the climbing season. So in good conditions Fyfe, Clark and Simpson set out via the Noeline Rock for a bivouac which had already been established and which gave a good approach to the climb. Early morning on 11 March 1911 Fyfe and Clark again began climbing together on Mt Cook — the first occasion since their success in 1894. The passage of time had not diminished their enthusiasm and skill, and the party made fast progress on the steep rock.

The Hooker Glacier follows up to where the rock ridge joins Mt Cook's western face with a large schrund near the edge of the rock. Beyond this a steep but firm rock rib leads to the top of the ridge. Fyfe's ability to climb where there were few holds now came into full play and they ascended the ridge quickly. About two-thirds of the way up the mountain they encountered a section of loose and shattered rock. Ahead lay snow and ice and the final slope, and they began cutting steps. The sky was still clear on this stretch and this gave them an outstanding vista over the surrounding peaks, valleys and lakes. They soon reached the

Alex, left, and Peter Graham, successors as guides to Tom Fyfe and Jack Clark, pose with Freda Du Faur, the outstanding Australian climber.
Source: Peter Graham Collection.

summit — Tom Fyfe's third ascent, and again he had accomplished it with his characteristic speed and skill. After spending some time on the peak they began the descent and completed it without accident or incident.

Somehow Fyfe managed to combine work, family commitments and climbing through into the next climbing season when, again with Simpson, he made an expedition into the Arrowsmith mountains that drain into the Rangitata River. Here good peaks abounded, and Mt Arrowsmith (8185 ft) was itself unclimbed. This time their good luck with the weather deserted them, however, and on 3 February 1912 they were heading out of the mountains just as H. F. Wright and Guide Murphy from the Hermitage were moving in. The two groups met at the 'Jumped-Up Downs', and Wright and Murphy went on to a successful first ascent of Mt Arrowsmith.[5]

Tom Fyfe's last climbing at Mt Cook came about in unusual circumstances. From the beginning of serious mountaineering in 1882 there had not been one climbing fatality in the area. In February 1914 an ambitious complementary traverse of Mt Cook was planned. One party was to ascend from the Hooker Glacier by Earle's route and another from Haast Ridge via the Linda. Meeting on top, each party would then follow other's footsteps down. Although it was carefully planned, each party had to rely on the success and timing of the other's ascent, and this made it a risky undertaking.

The Hooker party consisted of a Canadian, Otto Frind, his Austrian guide, Conrad Kain, and a Hermitage guide, William Brass. The three climbing from the Linda side were an Englishman, Sydney Locke King, and two Hermitage guides, Darby Thomson and Jock Richmond.[6]

The Linda party arrived at the summit quite quickly and spent some time there waiting for the Hooker party to arrive. By mid-afternoon they dared not wait any longer, and returned by the way they had come. The Hooker party, having encountered difficult conditions, did not reach the summit until later. On their descent they found that that the Linda party had been overwhelmed by a massive avalanche on the Linda Glacier, probably loosened by the late afternoon sun.

The loss of the experienced Darby Thomson and the younger Jock Richmond left the Hermitage short staffed. Tom Fyfe immediately offered Peter Graham his services. The climbing season was at its peak, with parties to be guided and huts to be stocked. When the numbers had dwindled, Fyfe — then aged nearly forty-four — and Conrad Kain did some climbing together.

By 1914 most of the great peaks of over 10,000 feet had been

The second Hermitage, erected in 1914 to cater for the expanding tourist trade. In the same year the original Hermitage was destroyed by a flood from the Mueller Glacier.
Source: New Zealand Publicity Studios

climbed, and the focus for new ascents turned elsewhere. Samuel Turner and guides from the Hermitage had climbed many of the 9,000 foot peaks in the Mueller Glacier area, but there were still a number of virgin summits near the Hermitage. Among the more attractive were some rocky spires overlooking the Hooker Glacier between the Copland Pass and Mt La Perouse. Raureka Peak and Dilemma drop sharply into the Copland Glacier, and offered the prospect of excellent rock-climbing on the Banks Range. Beatrice, the East Peak of Dilemma, had been climbed by Hugh Chambers, Beatrice Holdsworth and Peter Graham on 28 January 1914, but the other peaks in the area remained unclimbed.

On 26 March 1914 Fyfe and Kain left for the Hooker Valley, setting up camp at the end of the Hooker Track. The view from here is striking — a myriad of peaks tower above, and Mt Cook is especially dominant. Rising early next morning, they decided first to climb Raureka Peak, which stands out as a fine wedge-shaped mountain on the Main Divide. They quickly made their way up the eastern rock face from the Hooker Track and gaining the base of the south ridge, they soon made the summit. With time to spare they decided on a traverse. Making their way down the north ridge and along the Main Divide, they ascended Beatrice (8,835 ft). Having scaled two peaks in one day, two of them virgin ascents, Fyfe

Mt Unicorn, Mt Dilemma and Raureka Peak, from the Copland valley. In March 1914 Tom Fyfe and Conrad Kain ascended these summits from the Hooker Glacier behind the ridge.

Photo: Gottlieb Braun-Elwert, Alpine Recreation (Canterbury) Ltd.

and Kain, elated, returned to the valley floor by way of their ascent.

As it turned out, those climbs were Fyfe's finale as a mountaineer. The First World War was only months away.

The early years of his marriage had been difficult for him, family responsibilities competing with both the love of climbing and working away from home. In 1915 the family moved to Auckland, where he was again employed in the expanded business of his uncle, James Craigie. By 1916 the war was going badly, and with heavy casualties overseas and volunteering dwindling at home, conscription was introduced. The upper age limit was forty-four, and men with wives and families got exemptions.

But for Fyfe, then nearly forty-six, the chance for adventure was still strong, so he enlisted and was posted to the 1st Battalion of the Auckland Regiment. On 10 March 1916 he arrived at Trentham military camp having given his year of birth as 1872 instead of 1870, thus becoming one of the many '43 and 44-year-olds' in the New Zealand Expeditionary Force. His unit left for France in September 1916, and by 14 October they were on the Somme where Fyfe was in action. However, wet and cold in the trenches, his old leg injury flared up again within two months. He became immobile and was transferred in turn to a clearing station, to a field hospital and then to the New Zealand Convalescent Hospital at Walton-on-Thames. Sent home to Auckland on the troopship *Ironic* in July, he was finally discharged in October 1917.

It was not a happy homecoming. Shortly after his return the family was stricken by the tragic death of Clyde, the younger daughter. This, together with his war experience, had a profound effect on Tom Fyfe. He never lost his love of the outdoors, but he now spent more time at home than previously. He was known as a quiet easy-going person, uncomfortable under authority and unwilling to impose it on others.

In 1918 the Fyfes moved to Blenheim where Tom worked at his trade through the 1920s. The sons, Kenneth and Malcolm, lived with their parents, but Lila, the older daughter, had already moved to Wellington and eventually to Australia. During the Depression Tom did some gold-mining near

Conrad Kain at Malte Brun Hut. Because of his Austrian nationality, he was unwelcome at Mt Cook at the outbreak of war, and he soon left New Zealand.

Source: New Zealand Alpine Club archives, Hocken Library.

Mary Ann Fyfe (née Peake), Tom Fyfe's wife.

Source: Dale Fyfe and T.M. Fyfe.

Blenheim and on the West Coast. On one trip at the age of sixty he went back into the Callery and climbed some of the saddles that overlook the Whataroa River, the scene of that desperate day in 1897 when he and Malcolm Ross had had such difficulty crossing it.

The Fyfes moved to Hastings in 1930, where they lived, quite by chance, close to Tom's old friend and climbing mate, George Graham. In his later years, when he was not caring for Annie who suffered from asthma, Tom Fyfe enjoyed reading, walking and cycling. In 1947 he died of emphysema, aged seventy-seven. He is buried in the Hastings cemetery.

Tom Fyfe's grave in the Hastings cemetery. The age shown (75) reveals his successful attempt to be eligible for war service

Source: T.M. Fyfe

1. Public Works Register of Service 1906, (Wellington: National Archives).
2. W. Vance, *High Endeavour*, (Timaru: The author, 1965), p.172.
3. *The Press*, 16 January 1909.
4. Ibid.
5. H. C. Wright, "First Ascent of Mount Arrowsmith," *NZAJ*. Vol. 3, No. 10, (March 1921): 49-52.
6. J. Wilson, *Aorangi*, p.137.
7. Service history of Private Thomas Camperdown Fyfe, No. 14094. Ministry of Defence.

CONCLUSION

What did Thomas Camperdown Fyfe contribute to New Zealand mountaineering? It is almost inevitable that he will be best remembered for having led the first ascents of both the Middle and High Peaks of Mt Cook and the first traverse of its High Peak eleven years later. He has had some recognition as having made the first ascent of a 10,000 foot peak in New Zealand, Malte Brun, but it is less well known that he did so by its steep, demanding west face and in a climb that, exceptionally for the times, was done solo.

But he also has to his credit a number of other significant pioneering activities in the mountains of the South Island, some of which are not well known. He led the first ascents of a number of other major summits — The Footstool, Mt De la Beche, Mt Darwin and the North Peak of Mt Haidinger. Lesser but still noteworthy climbs were those that he did in the Remarkables, in Fiordland and others in the Mt Cook region. His active climbing career, which began in 1890, spanned twenty-four years, culminating in a third ascent of Mt Cook and in climbing Raureka Peak, another virgin summit.

In other related ways Fyfe's achievements in the Mt Cook region were significant for mountaineering in this country. His alpine expertise, combined with a number of professional guiding assignments that began in 1892, led to his appointment in 1896 as the first full-time professional guide for high climbing in New Zealand. He was also a pioneer of exploratory trips, notably in finding new alpine crossings to the West Coast over Fyfe Pass and Lendenfeld Saddle. These achievements, taken with his personal, individual skills on high peaks, put Fyfe in a class of his own.

In addition he made important contributions to mountaineering techniques and traditions. Almost entirely self-taught, he was always ready to look for alternatives and improvements. Sometimes this meant trying a different route when the way was blocked; almost always his assessments in such situations were extremely accurate. He was quick, too, to experiment with equipment. Early in his career he found that he could move faster and more safely on steep rock than on steep snow and ice if he changed from the usual hob-nailed boots to the rubber-soled sandshoes he always carried in his swag.

His physical strength and fitness was a valuable asset because it meant that he could endure trying conditions. And he was personally well suited to mountaineering in other ways as well. He had strong nerves, plenty of self-confidence and no fear of heights. His creative attitude to the challenges he met and his friendly personality were seen as positive attributes by others and made him both a good team member and an outstanding leader. His guiding experience would have contributed to the leadership he displayed on other climbs and the confidence he imparted to his companions.

Before Fyfe began climbing, no major summits had been reached anywhere in New Zealand; when he retired few remained unclimbed. To this day several of the routes he pioneered, such as the one used on the first ascent of Mt Cook, are regarded as difficult, demanding the best rock techniques, and they have been repeated only rarely. Moreover, the careers of noted alpine guides who succeeded Fyfe, such as Jack Clark and Peter Graham, owe much to the direct help he gave them and to the traditions and the professionalism that he exemplified as a guide himself. Fyfe can be credited with the founding of alpine guiding in New Zealand.

During his climbing career Fyfe's reputation was second to none. It remains to survey how his achievements have been evaluated with the lapse of time. The most significant of his deeds — the first ascent of Mt Cook — was briefly acknowledged in Reed's history of New Zealand, first published in 1945.[1] In the 1966 government publication, *An Encyclopedia of New Zealand,* [2] there are more references to him, and Temple in his 1969 book about New Zealand mountaineers gives still more detail.[3] But not all historians have been as knowledgeable or as generous as Temple. For example, in the second edition of his book on exploration published in 1959 McClymont mentions Harper and Ross and even Fitzgerald, but not Fyfe.[4] And Pascoe, in his well-known 1958 book, stresses, quite mistakenly, that the three who first climbed Mt Cook were neither 'professional guides or even experienced amateurs'. He gives good summary accounts of Fyfe's ascents of Mt Cook and Malte Brun, but although he lists him as 'Fyfe, Guide Tom' in the index, he does not take into account that before his ultimate triumph Fyfe had had considerable experience both as an amateur and as a professional guide.[5] Wilson focuses on Mt Cook in his 1968 book, and he fully acknowledges Fyfe's achievements on that peak, devoting a complete chapter to the first ascent and then a detailed account of the traverse.[6] Logan's 1990 book about the most notable peaks in New Zealand also gives due recognition to Fyfe in chapters about Mt Cook and Malte Brun.[7] The 1993 publication, *Mountains of the South*, written by Gordon and well illustrated by Rundle, gives a number of appropriate credits to Fyfe, even though his name does not appear among the few notables listed on the flyleaf.[8] It is regrettable that there is no entry for Fyfe in the second volume of the *Dictionary of New Zealand Biography*, also published in 1993.

It is to be hoped that this biography of Thomas Camperdown Fyfe and especially of his climbing career means that his substantial contribution to New Zealand's mountaineering history will be better understood.

1. A. H. Reed, *The Story of New Zealand* 11th ed., (Wellington: A.H. & A.W. Reed, 1965).
2. A. H. McLintock, ed., *An Encyclopedia of New Zealand*, (Wellington: Government Printer, 1966).
3. P. Temple, *The World at their Feet*, (Christchurch: Whitcombe & Tombs, 1969).
4. W. G. McClymont, *Exploration in New Zealand* 2nd ed., (London: Oxford University Press, 1959).
5. J. Pascoe, *Great Days in New Zealand Mountaineering*, (Wellington: A.H & A.W. Reed, 1958).
6. J. Wilson, *Aorangi*, (Christchurch: Whitcombe & Tombs, 1968).
7. H. Logan, *Great Peaks of New Zealand*, (Dunedin: John McIndoe, 1990).
8. J. Gordon & J. Rundle, *Mountains of the South*, (Auckland: Random House, 1993).

GLOSSARY

abseil   to descend a steep rock-face by using a doubled rope coiled round the body and fixed at a higher point.

arête   narrow rock or ice ridge

belay   a rope secured to the mountain by an ice axe or piton (see below)

bergschrund (schrund)   deep gap between a glacier and the mountainside

bivouac (bivvy)   temporary shelter, or the camp made in such a place

col   saddle between two ridges

cornice   overhang of snow on a ridge

couloir   steep gully of rock or ice

crampons   framework of metal spikes attached to boot-soles for climbing on ice

crevasse   deep split in ice

glissade   to slide down ice or snow, using ice axe as a brake

ice axe   tool with a metal head comprising an adze and a pick for cutting steps in ice or hard snow

icefall   area of broken and contorted ice on a glacier where it moves over broken terrain

moraine   debris of rock carried by a glacier

névé   snow basin at the head of a glacier from which the glacier receives its ice

piton   peg or spike driven into a rock or crack to support a climber or a rope

swag   forerunner to modern pack: canvas sheet enclosing clothes and food with straps and carried on the back

Index

About the Author

John Haynes lives in Christchurch. As a sixteen-year-old, he began climbing southern mountains. Now he has combined his historical training, his fascination with mountaineering feats of the past and his own climbing and guiding experience to write this book. He has ascended many of the highest peaks in the Mt Cook region and elsewhere and knows intimately the rigours, the dangers and the satisfactions experienced by climbers.

John Haynes has a masters degree in Political Science from the University of Auckland. He taught history before taking up an appointment in the Office of the Ombudsman in Christchurch.